CONTENTS

CONTENTS

100

114

200

PAUL HARMER

75 YEARS OF FERRARI
Editor Chris Bietzk
Art editor Robert Hefferon

OCTANE & EVO EDITORIAL
Octane Editor-in-chief James Elliott
Email: james@octane-magazine.com
evo Editor Stuart Gallagher
Email: stuart_gallagher@autovia.co.uk
Autovia Limited
31-32 Alfred Place
London WC1E 7DP
Tel: +44 (0)20 3890 3890

OCTANE ADVERTISING
Group advertising director Sanjay Seetanah
Account director Samantha Snow
Dealer account manager Marcus Ross
Services account manager Doug Howard
Tel: +44 (0)1628 510080
Email: ads@octane-magazine.com
Advertising production Kerry Lambird

AUTOVIA MANAGEMENT
CEO Autovia Media Nicola Bates
Chief financial officer Benedict Smith
CEO Autovia Group Andy Oldham
Group advertising director Steve Machin
Publisher Holly Jerram
Editorial director Steve Fowler
Newstrade director David Barker

The Octane and evo brands are trademarks
of Autovia Ltd, 31-32 Alfred Place, London
WC1E 7DP. Company registered in England.
All material © Autovia Ltd and may not be
reproduced in whole or part without the
consent of the publishers.

LICENSING & SYNDICATION
To license or syndicate this content,
please contact Nicole Creasey.
Tel: +44 (0)20 3890 3998
Email: nicole_creasey@autovia.co.uk

Printed by Precision Colour Printing
Cover image: Alex Howe (alexhowe.com)

LOOKING IN THE REAR-VIEW MIRROR

Rewind 45 years or so to Cape Town, a seaside city with lovely weather, beautiful views and not much going on except political turmoil. What excitement there was in my young life was provided by my car-enthusiast father and his friends, who owned Astons, Jaguars, Porsches and vintage MGs and Bentleys – but no Ferraris. We heard that there were one or two in Jo'burg, 800 miles away, but they were not seen in sleepy Cape Town.

One day an old chap called Mr Schmitt passed away. While sorting out his estate it was discovered that he had a derelict warehouse, and a car was found hidden away inside. When it was hauled out of the darkness, it turned out to be a Ferrari Daytona. This caused a great commotion among the local car guys, none of whom had had any idea that the Ferrari existed. The secretive Mr Schmitt had apparently only ever driven the car surreptitiously at night.

My father piled me into his Porsche 356 and we raced down to the warehouse to take a look. The Ferrari was filthy, painted a dull green and missing its badges, but still it exuded glamour and power. I was bowled over, and I've wanted a Daytona of my own ever since. Today, as Ferrari turns 75, its cars continue to inspire awe and devotion, and in the pages that follow we celebrate some of the greatest achievements of a marque that has made so much motoring magic.

Robert Coucher, founding editor, *Octane*

THE INTELLIGENT ALTERNATIVE FOR FERRARIS OF YESTERDAY, TODAY AND TOMORROW

Financing the Dream

Operating throughout the authorised Ferrari network, Ferrari Financial Services can tailor a range of financial products offering both private and corporate clients an original and highly favourable way of purchasing any pre-owned Ferrari.

Our financial products are aimed at cars which retain their value over time and are applicable to all Ferrari models, regardless of age.

Contact our team today to discuss your next Ferrari purchase.

Steven McLaren
+44(0)7739 035782
steven.mclaren@ferrari.com

Kevin Briggs
+44(0)7500 074390
kevin.briggs@ferrari.com

Nick Simmons
+44 (0)7887 724992
nick.simmons@ferrari.com

Ferrari Financial Services GmbH
275 Leigh Road, Slough
Berkshire, SL1 4HF
www.ferrarifinancialservices.com

FINANCIAL SERVICES

Enzo
FERRARI

Doug Nye tells the epic story of the man who
rose from humble beginnings to build an empire

Portrait Ferrari

'**D**o us a story on Enzo Ferrari,' they said. Of course, the proposition is quite simple, but how can one adequately address the single most significant motor racing personality of the 20th century in just a few magazine pages? The sin will be omission; there's too much to tell to avoid it.

Enzo Anselmo Giuseppe Maria Ferrari came from a lower-middle-class family of Modenese artisans. He spoke Modenese dialect, blunt and to the point. But he was also bright, astute and ambitious – and he had a backbone of spring steel, forged through early adversity, sickness and loss. This was the man who would become a personality of global stature, who would eventually have kings, princesses, dukes, film stars and captains of industry clamouring for an audience at his Modena office or his Maranello factory. He throughly enjoyed keeping them waiting.

The cars his company built were exotic and especially exclusive. The more wealthy or famous you were, the more Enzo, always a canny marketeer, played the role of having to be persuaded to let you buy one. A close acquaintance of his confirmed for me recently how *Il Drake*, as the Italian press came to call him, never lost his fascination with manipulating the great and wealthy. 'He liked to see them dancing to his tune, yet once they offered enough money, he would sell them anything. He always loved to make the big score. The wealthy might have got what they wanted and gone away smirking, but they had left their money with him…'

Enzo's mercantile abilities were central to Ferrari's success, but more important still was his skill as a manipulator. He was a God-gifted exploiter of other people's talents, and for decades he had an almost unerring eye, particularly for an engineer who would contribute to the Ferrari legend. And before that engineer's potential had been used up, Enzo would have another groomed and waiting in the wings, ready to take over.

ENZO'S HOME TOWN of Modena, located at the foot of the Appenines on the southern edge of the Po Valley floor, has long been famed for its craftsmen. Skilled metalworkers, foundrymen, pattern- and toolmakers and designers abound. For decades most of them were willing to work absurdly long hours for laughably low wages. A job well done was considered its own reward. His father, Alfredo, ran a modest metal fabricating business and had two sons: Alfredo, born in 1896, and Enzo, born on 18 February 1898.

Enzo was ten when Alfredo Snr took the boys to Bologna to watch the Coppa Florio road race. Felice Nazzaro won in a Fiat. The next year, Enzo watched the local sprint meeting on the Navicello Straight. Motor cars and racing excited him greatly. When Italian-American Ralph De Palma won the 1915 Indy 500, Enzo saw his photograph splashed in the sporting press and declared, 'I'm going to be a racing driver!'

His formal education was sketchy, but his teenage years were spent in self-education; he was always a keen reader, and from his books he absorbed an understanding of his fellow man. In the 1980s, when I asked Ferrari's long-serving chief engineer Mauro Forghieri (interviewed on page 108) what he considered to have been the Old Man's greatest attribute, he thought hard before replying, 'An understanding of human weakness.' He would ruthlessly capitalise upon any chink in a talented man's personality or character.

In 1916, Enzo's father and brother both died, and in 1917 Enzo was conscripted into the Italian Army. He quickly contracted the killer flu that took more lives in 1918 than the Great War itself, and barely survived, suffering ever after from 'a weak chest' – a malady that he would brandish unselfconsciously when it suited him, to secure any perceived advantage.

By his own account, Enzo wound up alone in the immediate aftermath of the war, but this conveniently ignores his continuing closeness to his mother, Adalgisa, who provided an anchor in his young life. Rejected by Fiat in Turin, he got a job collecting truck chassis for a dealer named Giovannoni and delivering them to a coachworks in Milan, where they were bodied as more in-demand passenger vehicles. Thus he got to know and be known by the motoring men of both great cities. One was Ugo Sivocci, who was a proper test driver for CMN. He fixed Enzo a full-time job there as a test driver and, on 23 November 1919, Enzo drove a CMN in Italy's first post-war sporting event, the Parma – Poggio di Berceto hillclimb. He came fourth in his class, and six weeks later he managed ninth in the first post-war Italian road race, the Targa Florio.

For the 1920 Parma – Poggio di Berceto, held in May of that year and after Sivocci had moved to Alfa Romeo, Ferrari bought himself an old 1914 GP Isotta Fraschini. He drove it to third place, then raced it again at Mugello and in the Consuma hillclimb. Sivocci then arranged for him to come and work at Alfa Romeo, where Enzo became both a regular team driver in minor-league events and right-hand man to Nicola Romeo's closest aide, Giorgio Rimini. When Alfa Romeo ran stripped production cars in the 1920 Targa Florio, Enzo drove one home in second place. Over the next three years he would drive only for Alfa Romeo, save for one outing in a Steyr, of all things, at the 1922 Aosta – Gran San Bernardo hillclimb. During this period, he became Rimini's Mr Fixit.

At the time, Fiat ruled Grand Prix racing, its Torinese experimental shop at the cutting edge of automotive technology. When Sivocci was killed in the prototype Alfa Romeo GPR (or 'P1') during practice at Monza ahead of the 1923 Italian GP, Rimini persuaded Nicola Romeo that they should headhunt Fiat's design team. Ferrari was Alfa's chosen envoy, and through him the legendary engineer Vittorio Jano, among others, was lured to Alfa Romeo.

> '**The wealthier you were, the more Enzo played the role of having to be persuaded to let you buy a car**'

Meanwhile, Enzo raced mostly second-string cars, but he nonetheless recorded his first outright win, in June 1923 at Savio. In 1924 he took three big victories in a row, at Savio, Polesine and Pescara. The last of those earned him the minor honour of *Cavaliere dell'Ordine della Corona d'Italia*. He was later elevated to *Commendatore*, a title used popularly for decades even though Enzo explained it was a Fascist honour abrogated after the regime's defeat. He preferred to be called '*Ingegnere*', or 'Mr' or 'just plain Ferrari'.

His 1924 hat-trick of wins persuaded the Alfa management to nominate him as their fourth driver for the biggest race of the year, the Grand Prix de l'ACF at Lyon-Givors. Enzo practised there in the new, Jano-designed P2, but opted out before the race, fleeing home to Modena. He later explained that he'd suffered a nervous breakdown. The great journalist Giovanni Canestrini believed privately that 'He was just plain scared. The P2 was beyond him.'

It says much about Enzo's popularity that not a word of this was published, and that Alfa Romeo stood by him. Within weeks of Lyon, he was working as closely as ever with the team, though not as a driver; he didn't race again until 1927, by which time he was running a healthy Alfa distributorship in Modena. He won again at relative bush-league level. By then he had married a well-off Milanese girl, Laura, who travelled to all the races with him.

From top
After World War One, Enzo enjoyed some success as a racer before finding his calling as a team manager. His drivers included Tazio Nuvolari, seen here (centre, next to Enzo) topping up his fluids after the 1930 Cuneo – Colle della Maddalena hillclimb; and on the way to victory in the 1936 Vanderbilt Cup.

Left
Now here's a curio. In the 1930s, petrol shortages in Italy led to trials with cars powered by wood gas. These burned wood or charcoal or coal to produce a combustible gas. An Alfa Romeo *gasogeno* ran in the 1933 Mille Miglia, though very slowly. Enzo (far left) was not impressed.

'At his best, Enzo was a cool and cultured racing driver. During the 1940s and '50s, his own engineers rated his test-driving abilities quite highly'

Enzo's Modena premises attracted a clientele of gentleman racers, and at the end of 1929 he persuaded three of them, the Caniato brothers and Mario Tadini, to finance the creation of Scuderia Ferrari, which would prepare, enter and run their sporting Alfa Romeos. They could then just report at the right place on the right day and find their cars present and ready to race.

As a new chapter of Enzo's career began, another came to an end. He notched up his last victory as a driver in the Bobbio – Passo del Penice hillclimb on 14 June 1931, while his very last entry came on 9 August that year at the Tre Provincie road race, where he was narrowly beaten into second place after a long, hard battle with Tazio Nuvolari.

At his best, Enzo had been a cool, analytical and cultured racing driver. During the 1940s and '50s his own engineers would rate his test-driving abilities and his feedback quite highly. Behind the wheel of a road car, he was quick, safe and neat, almost to the end of his driving days. In 1931, ever the publicist, he made much of his retirement from racing and the sense of loss he felt. He had always promised Laura he would stop when they had children, and she had just told him she was pregnant.

The couple's baby boy arrived on 19 January 1932. Respecting family tradition they named him Alfredo, after the father and the elder brother Enzo had lost 16 years earlier. The affectionate diminutive of Alfredo is 'Alfredino', and hence the Old Man's firstborn son came to be known as Dino Ferrari.

The same year, Alfa Romeo's factory racing outfit ceased activities due to financial pressures, presenting Enzo with the opportunity to manoeuvre his fledgling organisation into the position of a quasi-works team. From mid-1932 until 1937, the Scuderia became 'Alfa Romeo Racing', and Enzo's longstanding interest in journalism (as a teenager he had contributed Modena FC match reports to the *Gazzetta dello Sport*) found an outlet in the form of the Scuderia's magazine. Enzo frequently published glowing profiles of the race organisers with whom he dealt, a ploy that fostered close relationships from which the Scuderia undoubtedly profited.

But this happy time came to an abrupt end in 1934 with the emergence of the state-sponsored German racing teams from Mercedes-Benz and Auto Union, which quickly rose to dominate Grand Prix racing, scooping up all the big prize money. Unable to compete with the *TransAlpini*, as he called them, Enzo looked to earn elsewhere.

FERRARI

In 1935, two twin-engined Alfa Romeo Bimotore Libre cars were built in his Modena premises, but their success was limited. Nuvolari scored a shock win in a Scuderia Alfa at the 1935 German GP, but it was a one-off. In 1937 Enzo masterminded the creation of a 1.5-litre supercharged car to race in the Vetturetta class – the Formula 2 of the day – and this emerged from his Modena works as the Alfa Romeo 158 Alfetta. But Alfa's new president, Ugo Gobbato, took his company's racing programme back in-house for 1938, and the Scuderia in Modena was wound up. Enzo could only briefly stomach being *Direttore Sportivo* at the new Alfa Corse HQ in Milan, where he was always being watched by senior management. With his style emphatically cramped, he walked out late in 1938.

WHEN ENZO LEFT Alfa Romeo, one condition of his severance agreement was that he would neither build nor race cars under his own name for four years, so he set up a precision machine shop in his old Scuderia HQ on Modena's Viale Trento Trieste and called the new business Auto Avio Costruzioni. It was there, around Christmas of 1939, that he was visited by the son of the late Alfa Romeo works driver Antonio Ascari.

Young Alberto Ascari and his aristocratic friend, the Marquis Lotario Rangoni, wanted Enzo to build them sports cars capable of competing in the 1500cc class of the upcoming short-circuit Mille Miglia at Brescia. Fiat was

offering attractive bonuses to those who performed well with Fiat-based cars, so Enzo and AAC produced two '815' cars, each powered by a Fiat-derived 1500cc straight-eight. At Brescia on 28 April 1940, Ascari and Rangoni ran quite well before retiring. But then Italy joined World War Two and Ferrari moved his company to Maranello in the Appenine foothills, manufacturing German-designed machine tools.

During the hostilities, Enzo performed a perilous balancing act of diplomacy, managing to stay on the right side of both Mussolini's Fascists and the communist pro-Allied partisans, who were especially active around Modena. As the war came to an end, he was already teeing up production of new road and racing cars, by this time free of his Alfa severance agreement and able to make use of his own name again.

Meanwhile, engineer Gioacchino Colombo, the principal designer of the 158 Alfetta, was at a loose end, having been laid off by Alfa and reputedly shunned for his support of the deposed and dead Mussolini. Loyalty to a dictator was just fine by Enzo… Colombo, he decided, was the man for him. And so, even while the bomb craters still smoked across the country, Enzo made his proposal for a post-war Italian sports car. He and Colombo agreed that a V12 engine offered the ideal combination of performance and long-term development potential, and the long history of Ferrari *dodici cilindri* power units began there and then.

'Lampredi's sun soon set. When he failed to deliver the goods in 1955, Enzo ejected him unceremoniously'

Through 1946, Ferrari's men developed their first V12s, which emerged in Italian national races in 1947 and achieved their first international race win at Turin that September, with Raymond Sommer driving a cycle-fendered 159 V12. Soon, Ferrari and the prestigious Mille Miglia would become linked in the minds of motorsport enthusiasts forever: the Prancing Horse cars would win the event no fewer than eight times between 1948 and 1957. It wasn't long, either, before Ferrari entered the Grand Prix arena. When Alfa Romeo took a sabbatical from racing in 1949, the Colombo-designed supercharged V12 Ferrari GP cars of Alberto Ascari and Luigi Villoresi began winning world-class races.

Having used up the genius of the butterfly-minded Colombo, and that of development engineer Giuseppe Busso to make the designs raceworthy, Enzo now turned to the tough and ambitious Aurelio Lampredi, who did brilliant work for Ferrari. In 1951 his unsupercharged 4.5-litre V12 cars broke the Alfetta's stranglehold on Grand Prix racing. 'I feel I have killed my own mother,' wrote Enzo, the theatrical language barely disguising his delight.

Lampredi's unblown 2-litre four-cylinder cars then carried Ascari to back-to-back Formula 1 titles in '52 and '53. Sports car victories piled up and and sales raged ahead. Enzo was on top of the motor racing world, bestriding it like a colossus. It took men of equal stature, and hardness, to cut him down. One such was Tony Vandervell, who made the Thinwall bearings that had provided a cure for the greatest frailty of the early Ferraris. When he and Enzo met, it was a classic case of flint cut flint.

For all that immediate success, Lampredi's sun soon set. When he failed to deliver the goods in 1955 he was unceremoniously ejected. A suitable replacement was found thanks to a stroke of good fortune: when Lancia stopped all racing activities, engineer Vittorio Jano (a colleague of Enzo's at Alfa Romeo) and the Lancia D50 that he had designed fell into Ferrari's lap.

From left
Enzo taking a keen interest in the construction of an early V12 engine; the first car to carry Ferrari's name, the 125 S (front row, left) emerged in 1947 and was soon winning races. This one was the Rome Grand Prix, run on a street circuit around the Baths of Caracalla.

ENZO FERRARI

Below and right
At the 1951 British Grand Prix, José Froilán González claimed his maiden F1 win – which was also the first for Scuderia Ferrari; in 1966 Ferrari was trounced by Ford at Daytona (and Sebring, and Le Mans) so a 1-2-3 victory in the '67 24 Hours of Daytona was especially sweet for Enzo & Co.

FERRARI

'When works drivers were killed at the wheel, Enzo mourned publicly, but continued racing undeterred'

On the road car front, Ferrari had established a proper production division in consort with stylist and coachbuilder Battista 'Pinin' Farina. The plan was to build and sell GT cars off the back of Ferrari's success in competition. Wins at Le Mans and in myriad other long-distance races had proven the 'unburstability' of Ferrari's designs, which also typically prioritised horsepower over handling; engine to the fore, chassis mere brackets to prevent the wheels falling off.

That design philosophy did not always make for 'easy' racing cars, and many drivers died at the wheel of a Ferrari – though it should be said that most of them loved their job and adored the cars that Enzo provided despite the fact that they could be difficult to control. When works drivers such as Musso and de Portago were killed while racing, Enzo was pilloried. He mourned publicly, but continued racing undeterred. As Phil Hill once put it, Enzo was always busily stoking the fire under the boiling cauldron into which every racing driver worth his salt would only too willingly jump.

Enzo experienced a personal tragedy in 1956, when Dino died from muscular dystrophy at the age of just 24. The Old Man agonised over his company's future, deprived as he was – he said – of an heir. But his very public and Latin grievings (no doubt fuelled by Laura, who was driven to distraction by Dino's death) abruptly stopped in the mid-1960s. Piero Lardi, the son of Enzo's mistress, Lina, and born at the end of the war, was working at Maranello. Reputedly Laura would occasionally try to track him down there, making the poor boy run for cover. Eventually, after Laura's death, Enzo publicly acknowledged Piero.

The aforementioned acquisition of Lancia's competition hardware and technology, which was facilitated by Fiat and cost Enzo nothing, helped to sustain Ferrari between 1956 and 1961. Fiat provided some cash, too, keen to halt the momentum of the resurgent Mercedes-Benz F1 team, which dominated in 1955 – but by 1963 Enzo was feeling the pinch.

He was being courted assiduously by Ford, however, and he used the advances of the men from Detroit to wind up Fiat before sending the Americans packing. With increased funding secured, he was then able to deny Ford the prize it coveted most, victory in the Le Mans 24-hour race, through 1965. The US giant sought revenge, of course, and eventually got it by smashing Ferrari at Le Mans between '66 and '68.

By 1969 everything was going wrong. Ferrari was making too few production cars to maintain adequate profitability. The Formula 1 team was struggling. The flat-12 engine intended to replace the V12 had bad teething problems.

Below
Enzo with Niki Lauda and Luca di Montezemolo, joint architects of the F1 team's resurgence in the 1970s.

Enzo approached Gianni Agnelli at Fiat and the younger magnate agreed to buy half of Enzo's company stock at a fixed annual rate, to be paid as long as the vendor should live. Enzo was doubtless determined that the purchase would cost Fiat dear…

Thereafter, Fiat was careful not to be perceived to be meddling; interfering with the Formula 1 programme, Enzo's great love, always threatened to provoke more public aggravation than it was worth. Enzo chaired a meeting at Maranello in the winter of 1987, and even at that late stage 'only one man was doing the talking', as one engineer who was present told me.

With the facilities, experience and technological back-up provided by Fiat, there was little excuse (at least until Honda, BMW and Renault entered the F1 fray) for Ferrari not to dominate racing for years on end. But over and over again, internal politics at Ferrari cost the team; the reality is that for many years Enzo repeatedly shot himself in the foot. After John Surtees won the Drivers' Championship in 1964, internal feuding chased the Englishman out of Maranello in 1966, and it would not be until 1975 that Ferrari, elevated by the talents of Niki Lauda and Luca di Montezemolo, would achieve such heights in Formula 1 again.

Enzo Ferrari was a great man, no question. He was also a difficult man, and a hard man. His liking for politics and plotting often backfired on him, but consider the load he shouldered in creating his company, the work ethic that saw him juggling in-house engineers and designers, outside chassis and bodywork suppliers, capricious customers, commercial concerns, driver contracts, the manipulation of sporting regulations, future planning, a visit from some king or Hollywood film star… Every one of his 16-hour working days was absolutely jam-packed for more than 70 years, almost until he died on 14 August 1988 at the age of 90.

For me, a moment recalled by Romolo Tavoni, Enzo's secretary during the 1950s, explains so much about the commitment, the intensity, the ambition of the man. 'You know,' Enzo sighed around 1953/54, 'it will only take three bank managers in Modena to all talk to one another, and we're f***ed!' Bravo, Ferrari. *End*

MEMORIES OF ENZO

The hard taskmaster
Giotto Bizzarrini Chief engineer (1957-1961)

'One morning Ferrari stormed into my office. "Bizzarrini," he said, "we have a warehouse full of spare parts for the 250 GT, an ageing model more and more difficult to sell. We can't afford to lose all those parts. Invent something to use them. You have 30 days or you're fired." Then he left.

I knew very well that he would have kept his promise, and I went straight to work on something new. The project became the 250 GTO. It originated from his threat and from my need of a salary: I had the mortgage on my house to pay and I couldn't afford to lose my job!'

The ruthless streak
Romolo Tavoni Team manager (1950-1961)

'Professionally, I grew up at Ferrari. When Enzo Ferrari hired me on 26 January 1950, he started to create me. I was the Scuderia secretary, and also his personal assistant, managing his working and private life. When he fired me in 1961, I was a manager and my mistake was undersigning, as every other manager did, a letter asking him to keep his wife away from the company. She had become unstable after Dino's death.

He fired us all – not because we had issues with Signora Laura, but because we asked a lawyer to write that letter. If we had talked directly to him, he never would have fired us. He was right and I was wrong, because he expected loyalty from us. Involving a lawyer in an internal company matter was like cheating on him. But he was ruthless: not only did he fire us, but he prevented us from finding new jobs around Modena or in the automotive industry for many years.'

Disobeying orders
Mauro Forghieri Technical director (1959-1987)

'We weren't rich, always struggling to keep to the budget. Ferrari didn't like old cars because he was always looking to the future. After a racing season, he always tasked Ermanno Della Casa, the company's trusted accountant, with arranging to destroy the old racing cars. Luckily – and not only because we would otherwise have lost many historical artefacts – Della Casa was not crushing the cars but was selling them to the most important clients.

He was not keeping the money for himself; he always gave it to the company, mostly the racing department, and we used it to do further development on the Formula 1 cars. Ferrari always knew everything that was going on, and I'm sure he was aware of this "violation of his orders" but accepted it – and most likely smiled seeing how it was benefiting the firm. But he never said a word about it.'

Conversing in French
Derek Bell Team driver (1968-1969)

'I'd been for a test at Monza and afterwards I went along to the factory to meet Enzo. We went for lunch over the road at the Cavallino and conversed in French. I don't know if he couldn't or wouldn't speak English. I hadn't signed yet and he was asking me about other drivers and was clearly interested in Rindt. Before I got home, my mother had received a telex for me asking me to go to Modena to sign the contract. She said, "If you do, you'll never walk into this house again." Enzo had a reputation for pushing drivers to the limit.

I flew out there and agreed to race F2, and F1 if I was good enough, for a fee of £250 a race, £500 in F1. I had a wonderful relationship with Enzo. He was very encouraging and he never did push me. We had many very enjoyable lunches and dinners together. I did two years for him. A year before he died I saw him again. It was very emotional.'

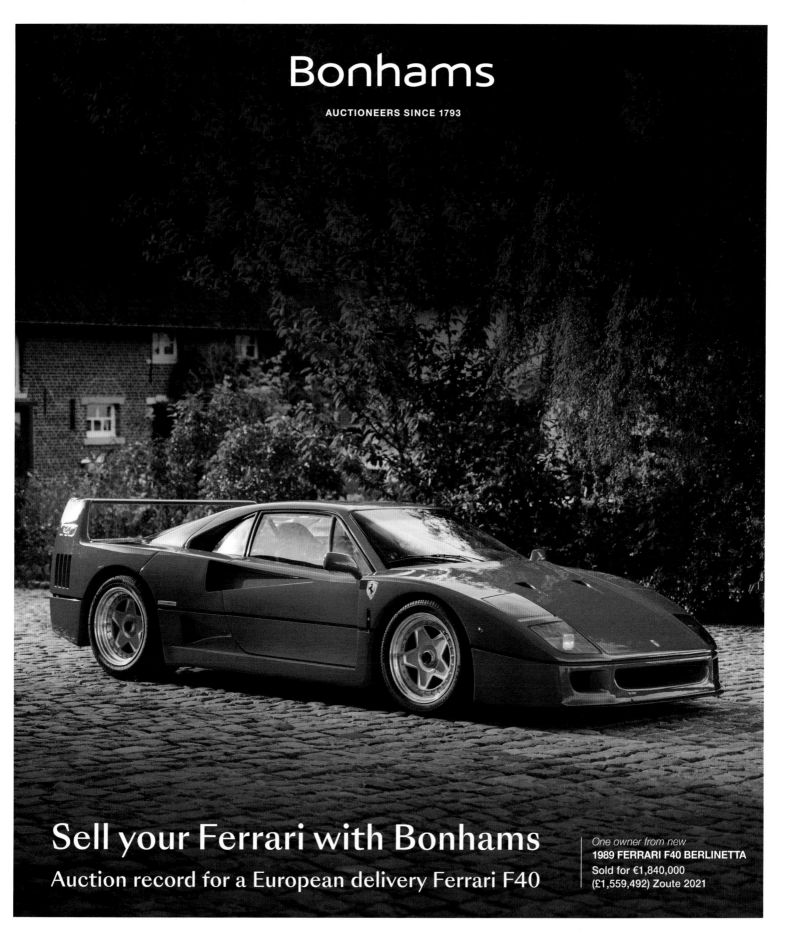

Bonhams

AUCTIONEERS SINCE 1793

Sell your Ferrari with Bonhams

Auction record for a European delivery Ferrari F40

One owner from new
1989 FERRARI F40 BERLINETTA
Sold for €1,840,000
(£1,559,492) Zoute 2021

ENQUIRIES

UK
+44 (0) 20 7468 5801
ukcars@bonhams.com

Europe
+33 (0)1 42 61 10 11
eurocars@bonhams.com

USA
+1 212 461 6514 - East Coast
+1 415 391 4000 - West Coast
usacars@bonhams.com

Catalogue subscriptions
+44 (0) 1666 502 200
subscriptions@bonhams.com

bonhams.com/motorcars

Prices shown include buyer's premium. Details can be found at bonhams.com

TOM HARTLEY JNR

EXQUISITE CLASSIC & PERFORMANCE CARS

1958 FERRARI 250 TESTA ROSSA
Chassis No. 0704 TR

1963 FERRARI 250 GT LUSSO
Chassis No. 4849 GT

1955 FERRARI 500 MONDIAL SCAGLIETTI
Chassis No. 0424 MD

1963 FERRARI 250 GT SWB CALIFORNIA SPYDER
Chassis No. 4121GT

1975 FERRARI 312T
Chassis No. 023

1965 FERRARI 275 GTS RHD
Chassis No. 07681

1985 FERRARI 288 GTO
Chassis No. 55713

1990 FERRARI F40
Chassis No. 086229

HERE ARE JUST SOME OF THE FERRARIS WE'VE SOLD IN RECENT YEARS

1968 FERRARI 275 GTB/4
Chassis No. 10803

2018 FERRARI LAFERRARI APERTA
Chassis No. 230938

1973 FERRARI DINO 246 GT CHAIRS AND FLARES
Chassis No. 06646

1953 FERRARI 250 MM BERLINETTA
Chassis No. 0310 MM

1967 FERRARI 330 GTS
Chassis No. 9655

1962 FERRARI 250 GT SWB
Chassis No. 3337 GT

1992 FERRARI F40
Chassis No. 093363

1973 FERRARI DINO 246 GTS
Chassis No. 06874

1966 FERRARI 275 GTB/C
Chassis No. 09041

Telephone: **+44 (0)1283 761119**

TOM HARTLEY JNR

EXQUISITE CLASSIC & PERFORMANCE CARS

1965 FERRARI 275 GTB/C
Chassis No. 07545

2002 FERRARI F2002
Chassis No. 220

1962 FERRARI 250 GTO
Chassis No. 3527 GT

1967 FERRARI 365 CALIFORNIA SPIDER
Chassis No. 09849

2014 FERRARI LAFERRARI
Chassis No. 200767

1967 FERRARI 275 GTB/4
Chassis No. 10291

1991 FERRARI F40
Chassis No. 086989

**WHETHER A MODERN
FERRARI OR AN
IMPORTANT CLASSIC,
WE ONLY SELL THE VERY
BEST EXAMPLES**

2004 FERRARI ENZO 'SCHUMACHER'
Chassis No. 128779

1972 FERRARI 365 GTB/4 DAYTONA
Chassis No. 15981

1965 FERRARI 275 GTS RHD
Chassis No. 08007

1965 FERRARI 500 SUPERFAST
Chassis No. 6659 SF

1965 FERRARI 275 GTB/6C RHD
Chassis No. 07797

1973 FERRARI DINO 246 GT
Chassis No. 06184

1961 FERRARI 400 SUPERAMERICA SWB
Chassis No. 2809 SA

1962 FERRARI 250 GT SWB
Chassis No. 3463 GT

1985 FERRARI 288 GTO
Chassis No. 53319

1965 FERRARI 275 GTB/C
Chassis No. 07641

www.tomhartleyjnr.com

'He was a tease!'

Brenda Vernor, PA to Enzo in his later years, remembers the Old Man's sense of humour and kindness

Words John Simister **Portrait** Tom Strongman

'**IF HE CALLED** at three in the morning wanting a letter typed, you'd go. One Sunday he needed to talk to Bernie and he needed me as the interpreter. I couldn't just do it from home; it had to be the office, his office. You couldn't say no to Enzo.'

In the 1960s Brenda Vernor left Croydon for Italy, which has been her home ever since. She initially worked as an au pair, but eventually became Enzo's PA and his conduit to potential new drivers, to Bernie Ecclestone, to anyone who didn't speak Italian but could manage English. Few people worked more closely with the Old Man.

'I first met him through Mike Parkes,' she recalls. The Scuderia Ferrari driver lived for a time in the same house as Piero, Enzo's son. 'Piero was one of my students – I taught him English, and later his daughter and his grandson, too. Mike was looking for a secretary and I started helping him in the evenings, so I saw Enzo often, and sometimes I kept his mother company.' She continued to work for Mike Parkes until August 1977, when he was killed, aged just 45, in a road accident outside Turin. Two months after that she was offered a job by Enzo.

'If he wanted something done now, you had to do it, but I got on very well with him, and he was thoughtful to his staff. I remember that one of the designers had a brain tumour and couldn't get a doctor's appointment, so Enzo called the consultant, paid for the treatment and the man recovered.

'I wanted to go away one weekend and take the Friday off. I had to ask him, but I kept on putting it off. Finally, on the Thursday, I banged on the door. "*Avanti!*" So I asked the question. "*Depende…*" Total silence. Then, "Will you be wearing a bikini?" Well, maybe… "You can go if you promise to wear a bikini." He was a tease under that forbidding exterior.'

And as much as Enzo cracked the whip, the factory was a happy place. 'We were a family; we all worked together. In the evenings I'd take a couple of bottles of Lambrusco and a cake I'd baked into the race department, and I'd be there with them until 2am sometimes. You can't do that now. We used to laugh and eat, but the work would still get done.

'We were a family. I'd take a cake and a couple of bottles of Lambrusco into the race department and be there with them until 2am sometimes'

'I had to learn the Modenese dialect very quickly so I could talk with the mechanics, but it's quite easy – like Italian, but also similar to French in some ways.

'Sometimes I would go to the races. I went to Monza, Imola, and also to Canada and Silverstone. Once, Franco Gozzi [the PR man] wanted me to go to Silverstone with him, and I went even though the Old Man had said I couldn't. It was hell for a week after I got back!'

The last time Enzo was seen in public was at the unveiling of the F40 at the Maranello Civic Centre on 21 July 1987, and naturally

Brenda was there. 'It's a nice car, the F40, but my favourite is the 275 GTB/4.' Somewhat surprisingly, though, she's never driven a Ferrari. 'I see them every day and I hear the roar of the engines, but it's like eating the same beef steak. I drive a Peugeot 206.'

Brenda left the Ferrari company's employ on 31 December 1993, after which she worked part-time for Piero Ferrari in Modena, at his engine parts business. 'I stopped doing that in 1995, but I'm always busy. Ferrari has changed, though. When I visited the other day, they actually asked for an identity card…' **End**

THE FAME STARTED HERE

This Ferrari 166 MM is the only car ever to have won both the Le Mans 24 Hours and the Mille Miglia. James Elliott drives what many believe to be the most important Ferrari of all

Photography Drew Gibson

Sometimes it is important to establish a frame of reference. The Concours of Elegance at Hampton Court Palace is one of the very best events of its kind, and despite being a new kid on the block in relative terms, it is already spoken of in the same breath as Pebble Beach and Villa d'Este. The concours field is always awash with the rarest and most desirable cars on the planet, yet even among the amazing entries at Hampton Court there is a hierarchy.

In 2019 the event belonged to the Ferrari 166 MM, the seminal model that cemented Ferrari's position as a maker of road cars and helped the company to break America. In pride of place in front of the Palace was a small, carefully curated group of 166 MM Barchettas, each historically significant in its own right, but even among these there was a focal point, a star car – and it was this one. The centrepiece of the centrepiece at the UK's centrepiece concours.

As you will have gathered by now, chassis 0008M, or '22', is not just *any* 166 MM. It is *the* 166 MM. It not only secured Ferrari's first Le Mans victory in 1949, it also won the Mille Miglia the same year, making it the only chassis of any marque to ever win both events. Today, many argue that it is the most important Ferrari ever built. Back in 1949 there was not even an argument to be had.

Enzo Ferrari had an awful lot riding on the 166 MM. Having already proven himself to be brilliant at running a race team, he wanted to do more, to build a carmaking business that would benefit from the reflected glory of his competition successes. That business would then fund more racing, which would… well, you get it. In pursuit of his goal, Enzo had taken out sizeable loans from three of Modena's banks, and increased the size of his workforce. He had obligations to more people than ever before, including a second son, Piero, born in 1945.

The first cars that Ferrari built were either outright racers or uncomfortable road cars. These were not the building blocks of a brand identity, and in any event they were too scarce to make an impression on the car-buying public. First to wear Ferrari's badge was 1947's 1.5-litre V12 125 S, followed by the 159 S. Just two examples of each were built. Next came the more successful 166 and then, at the 1948 Turin Salon, Carrozzeria Touring showed the 166 MM.

'THIS "LITTLE BOAT", ON A BARELY TWO-METRE WHEELBASE AND WEIGHING 800KG, WAS A MIRACLE'

Dubbed 'MM' in honour of the Ferrari 166 S that had won the 1948 Mille Miglia, it was instantly nicknamed '*Barchetta*' ('little boat') by journalist Giovanni Canestrini. The styling, by Federico Formenti under a young Carlo Anderloni, supposedly gave a nod to the Allemano bodywork of the Mille Miglia winner, but even when you squint there is little similarity between the boxy 166 S and the flowing Barchetta with its groundbreaking, all-enveloping silhouette. Regardless of the inspiration, the MM gave Ferrari a 'design language' for the first time.

With a tubular frame, wishbones at the front and a live rear axle, the 166 MM was fundamentally a development of the 125, yet the little boat, on a barely two-metre wheelbase and weighing just 800kg, was a miracle. Not only was it a more pliable road car than its predecessors, it also made a more potent competition car. At its heart was Colombo's magical 1995cc V12, fed by a trio of 32 DCF Webers (for racing; the roadgoing 166 Inter had just one carburettor), pushing out 140bhp via a five-speed 'box and good for over 130mph. Despite the enormous cost of all this brilliance (the equivalent of almost $10,000 dollars in Italy; $15,500 in the USA), some 25 166 MM Barchettas were built, plus six Berlinettas. That was on top of all the other 166 variants – the S, the Spyder Corsa and the Inter. Critically, the 166 was equally at home on road or track. It completed the circle of Enzo's business plan in one model: build, race, sell, build, race, sell.

Competition success came quickly to the 166, Clemente Biondetti winning both the 1948 Targa Florio (with Igor Troubetzkoy) and the Mille Miglia (with Giuseppe Navone) in an S. But these early triumphs were eclipsed the following year when the 166 dominated all of Europe's blue-riband events. Biondetti won the Targa Florio again, this time in an SC with Carlo Benedetti, and then won the Mille Miglia – in our feature car – with Ettore Salani. Another 166 MM took victory at the Spa 24 Hours piloted by Luigi Chinetti and Jean Lucas, and if that win is seldom mentioned these days, it is only because a month prior to that, Chinetti pulled off one of the greatest feats in the history of endurance racing.

Ferrari sold 0008M to a 36-year-old British nobleman, Lord Selsdon – actually Peter Mitchell-Thomson, a 2nd Baronet. He paired himself with the man who arranged the sale, Chinetti, for June's 24 Hours of Le Mans. At the first running of the race since the end of World War Two, the Ferrari was pitted against cars with much larger engines. A Talbot was quickest in practice, and the 166 MM seemed to have no hope of an outright win, but Chinetti epically drove for all but 90 minutes (some say 20, but let's err on the side of caution) of the 24 hours and brought the car home in first place.

1949 Ferrari 166 MM
Barchetta by Touring

Engine 1995cc 60deg V12,
SOHC per bank, three Weber
32 DCF carburettors
Power 140bhp @ 6600rpm
Torque 117lb ft @ 5000rpm
Transmission Five-speed
manual, rear-wheel drive
Steering Worm and peg
Suspension Front: double
wishbones, transverse leaf spring,
hydraulic dampers. Rear: live axle,
semi-elliptic leaf springs, hydraulic
dampers, anti-roll bar
Brakes Drums **Weight** 800kg
Top speed 130mph
0-60mph 10sec

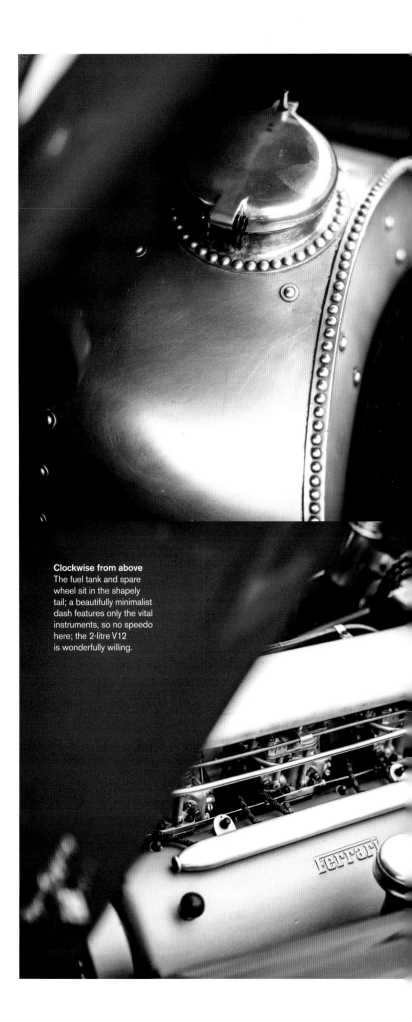

Clockwise from above
The fuel tank and spare
wheel sit in the shapely
tail; a beautifully minimalist
dash features only the vital
instruments, so no speedo
here; the 2-litre V12
is wonderfully willing.

The official line was that Lord Selsdon was ill. The lingering suspicion was that he scared himself so much in his first session that he refused to go out again. The truth? Probably somewhere between the two. He had, for the record, raced throughout the 1930s and '40s and had driven at Le Mans on two previous occasions, managing a fourth-place finish in 1939 in a Lagonda V12. Whatever went on in '49, his name is on the trophy – not bad for an hour-and-a-half's work, tops.

Also, crazy though it sounds, don't rule out the possibility that his brief stint may have been a tactical choice, one intended to give Ferrari the best chance of scoring its first Le Mans win. After all, Chinetti, an American citizen having stayed on in the US the after the 1940 Indy 500, was a formidable competitor with two Le Mans wins to his name already. He competed in every 24-hour race at Le Mans for nearly 20 years, knew Enzo personally from his days at Alfa Romeo, and would go on to become Ferrari's first US distributor and to found the legendary North American Racing Team. The dual-purpose 166 MM was the car Ferrari needed to build, but Chinetti, with his racing talent and sales skills, turned out to be almost as important to Enzo's business plan.

Chassis 0008M was displayed at the 1949 Paris Motor Show with the Le Mans trophy perched atop it, and the following year Lord Selsdon, reputed to have paid $17,000 for the car, sold it to Peter Staechelin in Switzerland. Staechelin raced it until 1952, and it next surfaced 15 years later with inveterate hunter of rarities Rob de la Rive Box, who passed it to Ed Bond in the USA. From Bond it went to Carl Bross and, after Bross's death in 1972, to Lord Bamford in the UK. It spent more than a decade with Bamford before it crossed the pond once more to reside with Tom Price, then Bob Baker. Finally, in 1996, it was acquired by Robert M Lee of Nevada, and there it has been ever since.

Lee was one of the world's foremost car collectors, with two Pebble Beach wins and a host of other trophies to his name. He was also a collector of rare firearms, an author, an explorer and a philanthropist. When he died aged 88 in 2016, his wife Anne, who for many years had been just as involved as her husband in their burgeoning Reno-based collection, made sure that the MM continued to be shown and enjoyed without disruption.

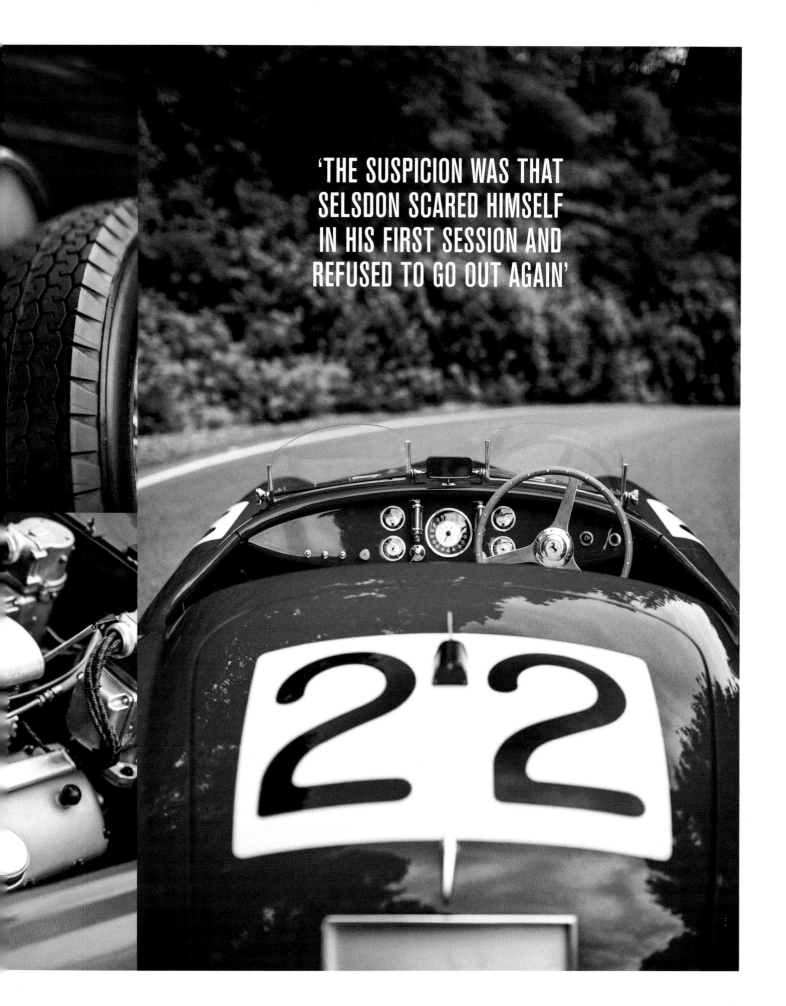

'THE SUSPICION WAS THAT
SELSDON SCARED HIMSELF
IN HIS FIRST SESSION AND
REFUSED TO GO OUT AGAIN'

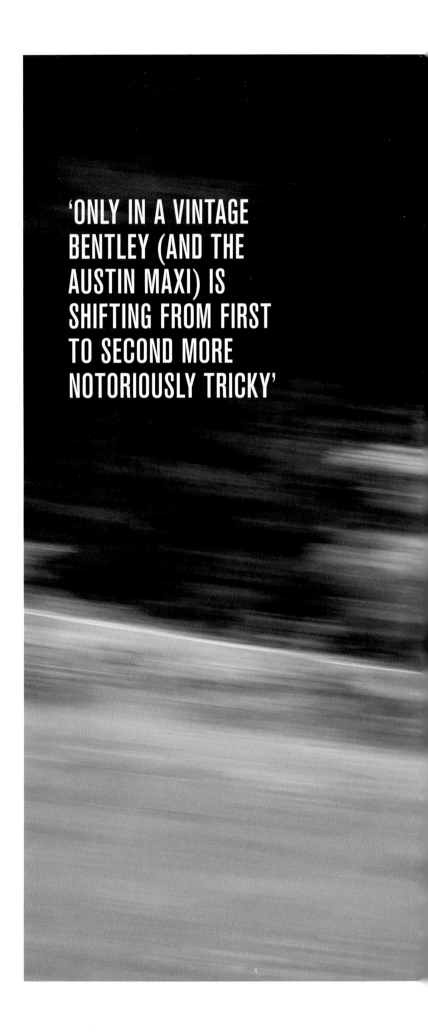

'ONLY IN A VINTAGE BENTLEY (AND THE AUSTIN MAXI) IS SHIFTING FROM FIRST TO SECOND MORE NOTORIOUSLY TRICKY'

While the Lees have always been generous in displaying their priceless piece of motoring history at shows, we cannot recall any magazine being permitted to track test the car, so when the opportunity was presented to us, we didn't need to be asked twice.

Some people nowadays dismiss the 166 MM as slightly gawky, but head-on, with that spotlight aiming at you and the purposeful transverse leaf spring visibly girded under the engine, it is gorgeous – petite but muscular. Plus, of course, there is that metalwork Zapata moustache tumbling either side of the egg-crate grille. This is the 'face' that inspired John Tojeiro, and in turn therefore the AC Ace, so it follows that here are the visual roots of the Cobra. My favourite view is from the side, though, watching the gentle wave of the wingline as it crests and dips over the door and wheels. Those wheels, chrome wire knock-offs equipped with Dunlop racing tyres, fill just the right amount of arch. It's not bad from the back, either. Who wouldn't be charmed by a tapering tail with a Le Mans lamp on it?

Open the featherlight door and drop into a surprisingly comfortable bucket seat. You're not too close to the steering wheel, nor is the wheel uncomfortably close to the dashboard, as in so many cars of the era. There is a reserve fuel tank in the passenger footwell, onto which the door gap sheds an healthy amount of light – very authentic. There is a similarly healthy amount of *Superleggera* frame on show, and it is surprising how thin the exposed tubes are (I'd guess 1cm, maybe 1.5), and how few of them there are. No wonder it's light.

Everything is beautifully presented, but the history of the car makes itself felt immediately. With the road screens removed, it's time to drive a Le Mans winner. Put in the key (just a slender rod of metal, really), push the button and wait while that urgent-sounding V12 goes briefly high-pitched before settling into its familiar staccato drumbeat, pulsing through the twin pea-shooters.

'Good luck with second,' whispers James Cottingham of DK Engineering (22's guardian while it is in the UK) with a slightly mischievous grin. The 166 MM's five-speeder is famously tricky, its higher-gear synchros being more of a theory than a reality and the first-to-second change trumped only by that of vintage Bentleys (and the Austin Maxi) for notoriety. We opt to avoid it, initially, when first to third is so much easier.

Some journalists think the repetitive and often low-speed process of driving for photography is a waste of time, but I revel in it. You learn so much about a car, how it would be in real life, its temperament. You learn that first gear is right up against the dashboard and that there is a fearsome drilled handbrake sprouting down from under the dash.

MOTORSPORT IMAGES

Above
Luigi Chinetti about to set out for
another epic stint at Le Mans 1949;
co-driver Lord Selsdon drove only
90 minutes of the entire 24 hours.

'THE CAR PITTER-PATTERS THROUGH SHARP CORNERS AND ATTACKS SWEEPERS WITH EFFORTLESS POISE'

You learn that the low-speed steering is not too cumbersome, that there is no wobble at all in the dash-mounted rear-view mirror, that reverse is difficult to discover but once found is never lost. And you learn that everything is as taut as could be, but equally it all feels so dainty and delicate that it's hard to believe the car could last 24 hours of all-out racing.

Of course, when the photography is over and there is time to really explore what this car is all about, you learn a whole lot more. Dainty and delicate become precise and responsive, nowhere more so than with the bulkhead-mounted throttle. There is plenty of space to let your feet play in the footwell without steering-column hindrance. Fifth is very civilised for cruising, but for all other occasions there is a rev-counter whose needle happily bounces up and down, though not quite to the inscribed 8000rpm on this occasion, for obvious reasons.

Eventually, I man up and head off round the back of the circuit to try and find second out of earshot. To my surprise it is there, a stern haul from first to second on the heavy lever bringing a satisfying connection and opening up whole new realms of enjoyment. With each shift it gets easier still, and I begin to think that this is not like other 166s. It's still fun to double-declutch, though.

More time with the 166 MM reveals it is not the baulky 'box that is the problem so much as the brakes. They are not unusual for the era, but that era was characterised by the fast-growing gap between the technology available to make a car go fast and the technology available to make it stop.

Steering is fluid and the balance on that short wheelbase and slender track is lovely, the MM pitter-pattering through sharp corners and attacking the sweepers with effortless tiptoe poise. The driver sits so low and contributes so much to the total weight that they become the fulcrum around which the delicious handling develops. Yet nothing tops the sweet bark of that gorgeous V12. It's at once smooth and threatening, with a terrier-like intensity and a labrador's eagerness to please.

This car is simply a masterpiece. If Selsdon was so ill that he couldn't drive it at Le Mans, he has my deepest sympathy because I can now comprehend what he missed out on – but if he consciously opted not to drive this car then he was the poorer for it. You would have had to prise me out of it. Actually, Cottingham did have to. **End**

THANKS TO *Anne Brockinton Lee, Clive Beecham and DK Engineering (dkeng.co.uk).*

THE TRUTH WILL OUT

Tony Dron reveals how detective work helped to confirm this car as the 1955 Monaco GP winner

Photography Matt Howell

A GENTLE BREEZE did little to reduce the heat blazing down on Monaco. It was 22 May 1955, and as a 37-year-old Maurice Trintignant took his place on the grid for the Grand Prix, he knew nobody gave him a hope in Hell of getting a decent result.

Way up ahead, reigning world champion Fangio was on pole in a new, short-wheelbase version of the all-conquering Mercedes-Benz W196, and in qualifying the Argentinian ace had scorched round Monaco's classic street circuit in a sensational 1min 41.1sec. Alongside him on the front row were Alberto Ascari in his works Lancia, and Fangio's Mercedes team-mate, Stirling Moss.

Lined up behind were Castellotti's Lancia and Behra's Maserati, both of them fast cars. Further back on the third row were even more of the impressive new Italian works cars – the Maserati of Mieres, the Lancia of the veteran Villoresi, and the Maserati of Musso.

Before they'd even started, then, there was an awful lot of traffic in front of Trintignant. His task, on paper, was indeed hopeless. Of the four Ferrari drivers on the grid, Trintignant was the quickest qualifier by 1.7sec, but that can't have been much consolation as he sat in the baking heat and stared at all the fast machinery in front of him. Ferrari was in the doldrums and 'Trint', as he liked to be known, was over three seconds off the pace despite his excellent qualifying performance.

Apart from the startlingly effective silver cars from Germany, it was obvious that Ferrari's Italian rivals, Lancia and Maserati, had moved well ahead of the Prancing Horse in 1955. Trintignant, though, was a proper racing driver who never gave up, no matter the odds. Over the next three hours the dapper Frenchman, who came from a prominent wine-growing family, demonstrated why he was never short of good drives all through his long career.

Although nobody has ever placed Trintignant in the same bracket as Fangio and Ascari, he was a true artist behind the wheel. After one race, he made the long journey home at very high speed, with a friend following behind all the way. I can't remember who the friend was, but the more important part of the story has stuck in my mind ever since I read it. As they were pulling into Trintignant's driveway, the man behind was about to inform his host that his brake lights were not working. Trintignant then coasted into his garage, applied his brakes to stop, and the two red lights on the back of his car blinked for the first time.

The start at Monaco in 1955 was on the other side of the pits from the previous year, and indeed its position today. It was on the road closer to the harbour – facing west, towards what was then the Gasworks hairpin.

When the flag fell, the Silver Arrows of Fangio and Moss streaked away, just ahead of Ascari and the street fight of all the rest. Trintignant was right in the thick of it, trying to avoid any damage in the madness of the first lap. He kept his wits about him as he watched, just ahead, young Castellotti briefly scrabble into the lead on the harbour front.

Ten laps in and the race had settled down, with Fangio and Moss out in front, followed by Ascari, Castellotti, Behra, Mieres, Villoresi, Perdisa and then Trintignant in the first of the Ferraris, still lying in ninth place out of the 20 starters. There were 90 laps of this to go, and he was already well down – but not out. At half-distance Fangio's transmission suddenly failed at the Station hairpin, leaving Moss in the lead from Ascari. By then the dogged and mechanically sensitive Trintignant had worked his way up to a surprising third place, and from that point on he was under constant pressure to stay ahead of the chasing pack. He was driving flat-out, unable to afford even the tiniest error.

Thirty laps later, everything happened at once. Moss, way out in front, suddenly found himself leading a trail of smoke. He dashed into the pits, but his race was over. At that moment

Ascari, knowing nothing of Moss's troubles, emerged from the tunnel and something went wrong at the chicane. This was the legendary moment that his Lancia darted sideways and shot through the air to fall into the harbour in a cloud of steam. Ascari's blue helmet was visible as he swam vigorously towards the shore before being hauled into a rescue boat.

Trintignant, now leading all the survivors, stroked it home for the last 20 laps to win by 20 seconds. In a masterly show of control through those closing stages, he remained unmoved in the face of intense pressure from the quick but erratic Castellotti in his fast Lancia. It was the Ferrari team's one and only World Championship race victory in the entire 1955 season. Farina, in a similar works Ferrari, finished third – a lap down.

The car seen here is the very same one that Trintignant drove in Monaco. Later in 1955, by which time the car had spent four seasons with the works team, Ferrari fitted it with a 3.0-litre 119 S (750 Monza-type) engine for Peter Whitehead, an English privateer rated by Enzo. He campaigned a series of ex-works Ferrari GP cars around that time, and notched up several major victories with this one in the Southern

Hemisphere in early 1956 before returning it to the factory. José Froilán González acquired it late in 1956 for South American races, scoring a string of wins over the next four seasons.

Still in South America, it was raced by others in 1961 and 1962, and Roberto Mieres drove it to its last recorded in-period win on 16 April 1961, in Argentina. By then it had been heavily modified with a Chevrolet engine and a totally different back axle arrangement.

Of 63 races up to that date it won 27, but its glorious past mattered less in the 1960s than it does today. As a worn-out old racer, dismantled and with little monetary value, it languished in South America for years. Thanks to American enthusiast Bob Sutherland and Englishman Peter Shaw, the remains were restored during the 1970s, in time to reappear at the Watkins Glen vintage race meeting in 1980. During that restoration, to reduce US tax charges, a brand new copy of the car was built and given to the Harrah Museum in the USA.

From left
The driver sits high in the 625 A, but the comfortable cockpit is a wonderful place to be – especially on a sunny day at Silverstone.

'Trintignant was under constant
pressure from the chasing pack.
He was driving flat-out, unable
to afford even the tiniest error'

IN 1999, WORD went around that a Grand
Prix Ferrari had emerged from a private
collection in Florida, and Alexander Boswell
jumped straight on a plane. The car he
inspected was described as 'chassis 3/0482, the
Peter Whitehead car' – but by then it barely
ran, bore little resemblance to Whitehead's
mount, and had been given a compromised
restoration. That night was spent in telephone
conversations with Ferrari enthusiasts around
the world, and the provenance was confirmed.
Boswell brought the car back to the UK.

Although it was obviously a genuine Ferrari
Grand Prix car, it was by no means certain who
had driven it in which races before Ferrari sold
it to Peter Whitehead.

Boswell was determined to get the car right
in every detail, but researching all those details
was no small task. A problem was that Ferrari
had more than one chassis numbering system.
There was one series for the customer cars
and a different one for the works racing cars.
Complicating matters further, these numbers
were sometimes changed by the factory. Back
in the 1950s, Enzo was not worried about
record-keeping; he was trying to win races and
run a business. Far from being fixed for eternity,
the number on a car's chassis was merely a
means of identifying it at a particular time.

When it was sold to Whitehead, the car was
given the chassis number of his previous
Ferrari, 0482, in line with the customer car
numbering system. During Boswell's research,
Ferrari expert Pierre Abeillon said to him:
'One day, you'll tell me that this is definitively
the Monaco car.' Remarkably, Abeillon had
managed to track the history of the car from
photographic records, crosschecking the exact
position and number of small screws and rivets
all over it. (In this respect, GP Ferraris of the
1950s varied like fingerprints.) Abeillon was
satisfied beyond doubt, but his assertion
surprised Boswell – not least because over the
years at least two similar Ferraris had been
described as the 1955 Monaco GP winner.

A close examination of the car was begun
prior to its complete restoration. As expected,
the stripped chassis carried the number 0482,
on a small plate welded to it. This was carefully
lifted, revealing another plate underneath it
bearing the number 2. That was not expected.
The car had always been regarded as works
chassis number 3, but nobody had ever noticed
that there were *two* plates underneath '0482'.
It was only when all three plates were revealed
that the car's original number, 3, was seen.

'Nobody had ever noticed before that there were *three* chassis plates on top of one another. Finally the car's original number was revealed'

The full story emerged: the chassis had been number 3 during the two-litre period of 1952-53, but changed to number 2 when it was converted to its 1954-55 2.5-litre F1 specification. The late Denis Jenkinson, that scrupulous doyen of motoring journalists, had been in the Monaco paddock and recorded that Trintignant's car was number 2. Reference to Jenks's actual notebook confirmed Abeillon's belief: it was indeed the 1955 Monaco winner.

A TRICKY QUESTION remained, though. To what specification should Ferrari 3/2/0482 be restored, anyway? It had seen so many configurations during and after its time as a works GP car. A book could be written on that alone, and it would not be a short work, but this is the essence of the story.

Trintignant's Ferrari at Monaco was not a bad car, it was simply out of date. It had originally been built for the 1952 season as the Scuderia's number 3 Formula 2 car, and with

Alberto Ascari at the wheel it won the first three GP races in which it was entered that year – the non-World Championship events at Syracuse, Pau and Marseilles.

At that stage, Ferrari was dominant in single-seater racing. In Formula 1, it had already risen to the top, and once Alfa Romeo pulled out, Ferrari had no effective opposition whatsoever. Consequently, in January of 1952, the FIA had suddenly announced that the World Championship would be run to F2 rather than F1 regulations that year. The news was reported in the British press as a 'Bombshell from Paris'. No doubt it came as a blow to the management teams at BRM and Talbot, but the FIA really had no choice. Alfa Romeo had gone, the BRMs had proved chronically unreliable, and the unsupercharged big Talbots were never going to be anything other than slow. With too few F1 cars in existence to form a grid, the only option was to run the 1952 World Championship with F2 cars.

Ferrari alone was prepared for anything, be it F1 or F2. With small-capacity V12 engines, Ferraris had ruled F2 racing for a couple of years and now this even faster car was unveiled for 1952. Designed by Aurelio Lampredi, it was described as the new 500 'Four' because it was a 2.0-litre, four-cylinder replacement for the very successful V12.

The engine was claimed to develop 180bhp at 7000rpm. British enthusiasts always claim Ferrari had noted the superior punch out of slow corners achieved by British four-cylinder HWM-Altas and French Simcas. Americans, on the other hand, tend to say that Ferrari had taken note of the Offenhauser Indy four-cylinder engine, and there's no doubt that its performance impressed Enzo and his engineers, if somewhat later on.

Interestingly, Lampredi's obsession with low weight and simple construction led him to experiment with a *two*-cylinder engine for the Ferrari works cars to use at Monaco.

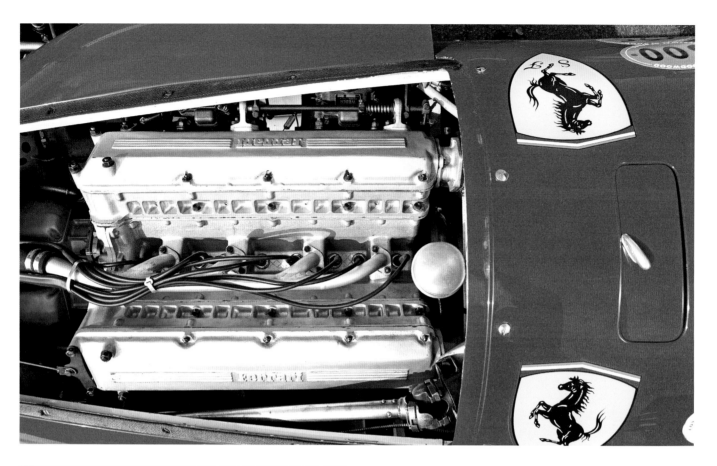

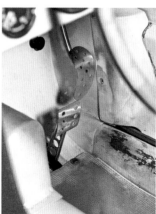

The 500 might seem conventional to us today but it was arguably the most successful Ferrari racing car of all time. The first World Championship GP of 1952 was the Swiss event at Bremgarten on 18 May. Piero Taruffi drove our feature car, and claimed both the win and the fastest lap.

Driving similar Ferrari team cars, Ascari won every round in the World Championship apart from the oddball Indy 500, which was included in those days even though it ran to totally different regulations. Ferrari drivers took the first four places in the 1952 World Championship and the result was much the same in 1953: using the same cars, Ferrari won seven of the nine rounds and Ascari was World Champion again.

It's often said that Ferrari grew so accustomed to winning that the team became complacent. There's probably some truth to that, but the criticism doesn't seem entirely fair, because a new Formula 1 car, the 553 'Squalo', was

Left
There's no V12 under those cam covers but instead a 3.0-litre four-cylinder, breathing through beautiful trumpeted Weber carburettors.

running in late 1953 in anticipation of the 1954 World Championship. The problem was that when the World Championship went back to F1 regulations in 1954, with a new set of rules specifying unsupercharged engines of up to 2.5 litres, the new Squalo struggled.

It was a good car in theory, particularly in terms of weight distribution, and it had an all-new four-cylinder engine, but its lap times suggested no progress whatsoever had been made. Lampredi was an engineer of enormous talent but the poor fellow must have been stretched to breaking point by his massive responsibilities. Any engineer in Formula 1 today would be astonished by the burden that rested on his shoulders alone, and it simply was not possible for one man to get everything right first time.

Meanwhile, the old 500 cars, including number 3, were updated to meet the new rules. Back in 1951, a prototype with an enlarged 2.5-litre engine had been run at Bari, and the 500 cars were altered in line with that prototype, becoming Ferrari 625s with a claimed 250bhp at 7500rpm. Our feature car was given works chassis number 2 for the 1954 season.

As the Squalo and the later 'Super Squalo' (555) still failed to threaten the competition from Mercedes-Benz, Lancia and Maserati, more radical changes were also made to the 625 for the start of 1955. The resulting car was named the 625 A, the 'A' denoting the location of its first race – Argentina.

Most obviously, there was a more aerodynamically slippery body with a lower nose and a wrap-around Perspex screen. Coil springs were fitted at the front because, surprisingly, the 625s had used transverse leaf springs all round. For 1955, the de Dion arrangement was retained at the rear but the leaf spring was moved above the final drive.

Other changes were made to our feature car at some point prior to the 1955 Monaco GP, including the extension of the wheelbase from 7ft 2.5in to 7ft 4.2in. The chassis was cut and lengthened towards the front of the cockpit. Quite why this was done – especially for the twisty Monaco circuit – is not known, but Trintignant's massive advantage over his team-mates suggests the handling was improved. Trint's 625 A was reportedly also fitted with a 270bhp Super Squalo engine and a five-speed gearbox for that race.

Ferrari 625 A (to 1955 specification)

Engine 2996cc four-cylinder, DOHC, two twin-choke Weber 58DCOA3 carburettors
Power 240bhp @ 6000rpm **Transmission** Four-speed manual, rear-wheel drive
Steering Worm and wheel **Suspension** Front: double wishbones, coil springs, Houdaille dampers,
anti-roll bar. Rear: de Dion axle, transverse leaf spring, twin parallel radius arms, Houdaille dampers
Brakes Light alloy drums front and rear **Weight** 635kg

Both the 625 A and the Super Squalo, in all their forms, failed to impress, and with the conspicuous exception of the Monaco win, the 1955 F1 season was a disastrous humiliation for Ferrari. If the Mercedes-Benz W196s failed to walk any of the races during that year, the Maserati 250Fs and the Lancia D50s were still there to leave the Ferrari team trailing behind.

The fact that the French, German, Swiss and Spanish GPs were all cancelled in 1955, following the Le Mans tragedy, simply saved the Ferraris from having their noses rubbed in the dirt any further. Late in the season, when Lancia ran out of money, that team's infinitely superior F1 cars were given to Ferrari. Aurelio Lampredi had been working on two new Ferrari F1 cars, a six-cylinder for the faster circuits and his two-cylinder for tighter circuits such as Monaco. That work was immediately abandoned and Lampredi left to join Fiat and the mainstream motor industry.

Above
Trintignant heads through Casino Square in the 1955 Monaco GP, sandwiched between Farina (Ferrari) and Mieres (Maserati 250F).

AFTER MUCH consideration, Boswell wisely chose to return his car to post-1955-season specification – in other words, to the state in which it was supplied by the factory to Peter Whitehead. The restoration took nearly two years, and much of the work was done at RS Panels in Nuneaton, where the body and chassis were returned to the correct shape with absolute precision.

His first race in the car was at Misano circuit in Italy, back in October 2002, and as I was there to drive in another race I was lucky enough to be able to watch the action. The 625 A had never been seen in Historic racing before, but Boswell emerged an impressive winner in a very exciting race. He told me that the car had incredible torque from low revs as well as plenty of top-end power. He also mentioned the excellent handling balance, the incredibly light but positive steering feel, and the great brakes that gave him the confidence to outbrake his rivals.

He was kind enough to allow me to drive the car on the new Silverstone GP circuit recently, during a Ferrari Owners' Club day. The driver

sits quite high up, even by 1955 standards, but the cockpit is well laid out and extremely comfortable. Hampered by a silencer to help meet the noise regulations that day, the engine stubbornly refused to perform properly at first. The car was still pretty quick and I was able to confirm everything I'd been told at Misano. The steering feels so alive and needs very little input, and the drum brakes in particular really are amazingly good, pulling the car up without the slightest twitch.

Then, after a stop for a new set of plugs, I experienced the full engine performance. The 625 A positively howled along the Hangar Straight, probably surprising the owners of several modern Ferraris as it shot past them. I got a lap and a half like that before the plugs started to miss again, and I won't forget it. By 1955, the 625 A may not have been a match for the relatively modern Silver Arrows and the latest cars from Lancia and Maserati, but the Ferrari delivers a fabulous driving experience. Maurice Trintignant must have been smiling to himself all the way home after that famous 1955 Monaco GP. **End**

FATHERS+SONS+FERRARIS

Saint-Tropez
13-15 MAY 2022

TIME TO APPLY

www.RadunoPadreFiglio.com

My first FERRARI DRIVE

On a surreal day in 1987, a young **John Simister** was ushered into a Grand Prix car

I HAD NO IDEA this was going to happen. *Motor* magazine, for which I then worked, had recently rediscovered Paddy Nevin, the artist who used to do action sketches at races for the magazine before World War Two. At the end of 1987, writer and historian Doug Nye thought it would be a great idea to take Paddy to Donington Park, so Paddy could see how it had changed and maybe capture our visit on canvas to illustrate Doug's story.

This Paddy gleefully did, despite suffering from cataracts at the time. Donington owner Tom Wheatcroft rose equally gleefully to the occasion and brought out a few cars from his collection, including Ferraris 125 and Squalo, plus a 312B from 1970. And, of course, they needed to be driven.

I'm not quite sure why I was along for the day, being the magazine's junior journo. Anyway, there were the cars, there was I, and Tom Wheatcroft said: 'Go out and enjoy yourselves.' So we did.

'I can still scarcely believe that the first Ferrari I ever drove was an ex-Grand Prix car'

First up for me was the oldest car of the five: the 125 Grand Prix car with a supercharged 1.5-litre version of Colombo's V12. It was bought new in 1951 by British racing driver Peter Whitehead (who won at Le Mans that year, in a Jaguar) and painted in mid-green.

I can still scarcely believe that the first Ferrari I ever drove was an ex-Grand Prix car, into which I was thrust having never previously driven a single-seater or a car with 12 cylinders. There ensued three laps – I think; it was all a blur – of Donington as I wrestled with swing-axle rear suspension that wanted to pitch me into a slither the minute I wavered in my cornering commitment, my learning curve barely tilting from vertical as I discovered, through necessity, the finer points of anticipating any need for opposite lock via the heavy, springy, mushy steering.

There were no heroics; I just didn't want to be the one who crashed. The V12 howled away but didn't actually feel all that powerful, which was probably a good thing. The long bonnet and the huge, wood-rimmed steering wheel brought to life childhood fantasies of what real racing cars might be like, and it was all over too soon.

Then, as dusk was settling over the circuit, and with no time even to fasten the seatbelts, I did three laps in a 1970 312B raced to victory by Jacky Ickx and Clay Regazzoni. I didn't even stall it, so friendly was the flat-12. My first two Ferraris. Wow. *End*

Below
A visit to Donington to inspire some artwork (top right) for *Motor* magazine presented John Simister (bottom right, then and now) with a chance to drive the ex-Peter Whitehead Ferrari 125.

25 FERRARI OWNERS TOGETHER FOR A WEEK

France
3-7 OCTOBER 2022

ASK FOR YOUR ADMISSION

www.HappyFewRacing.com

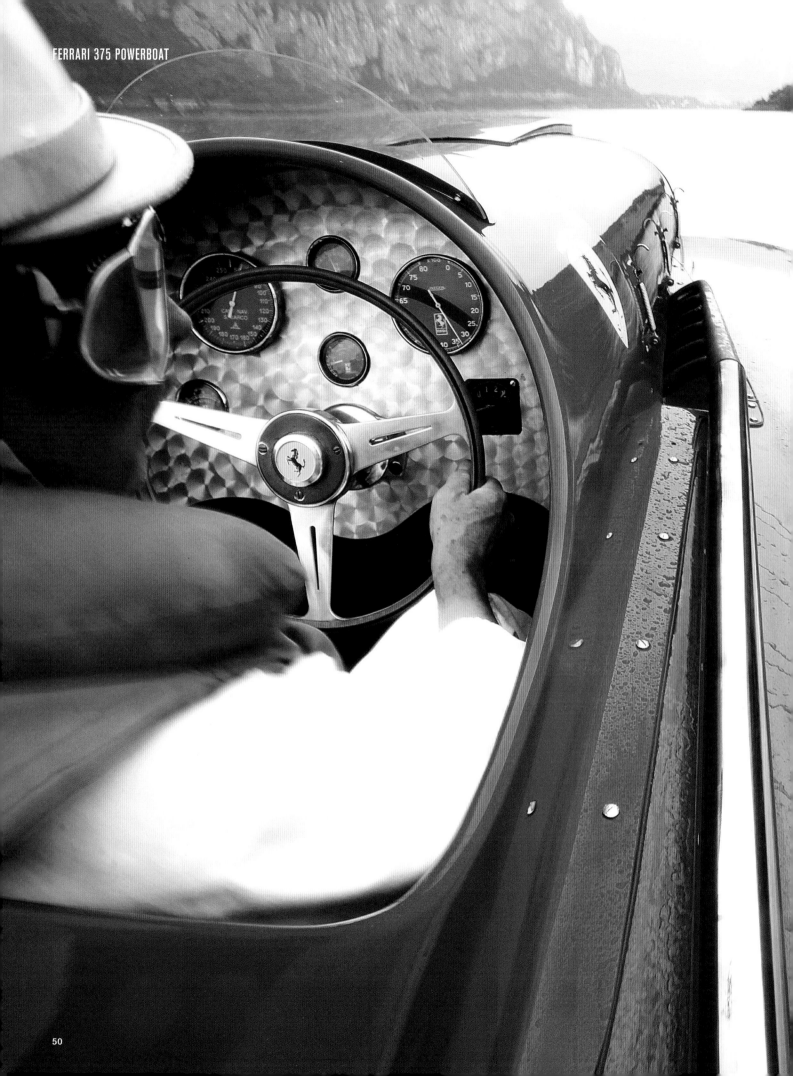

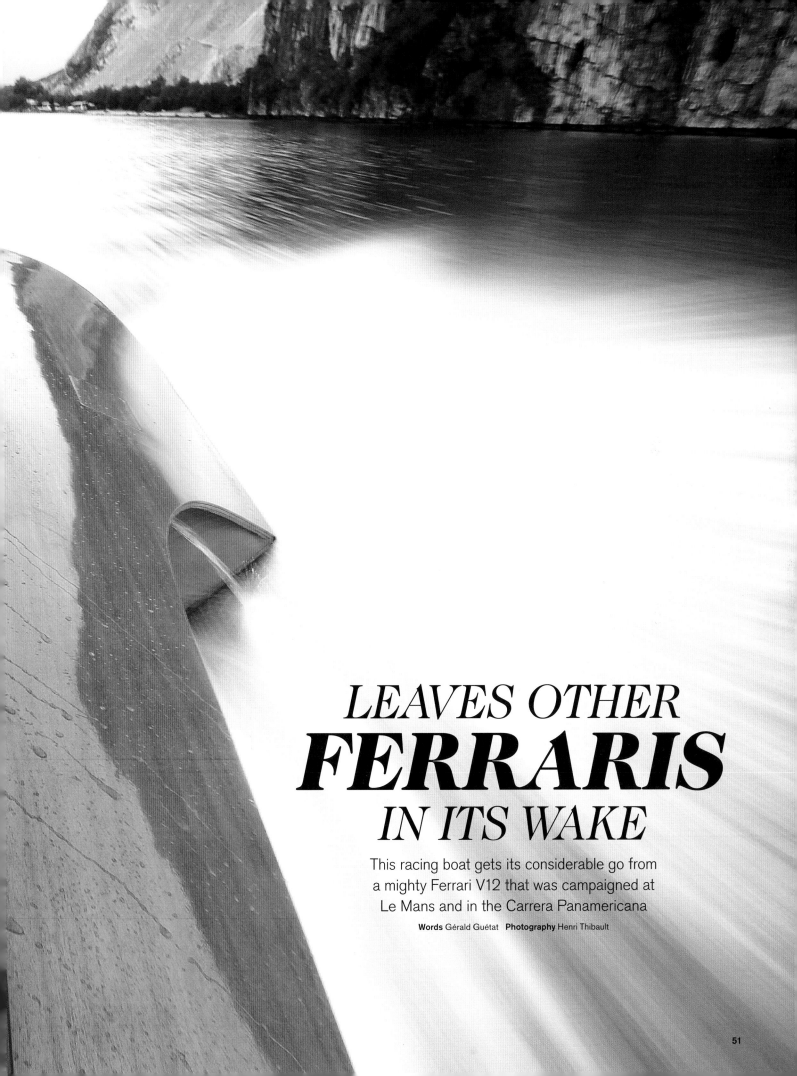

LEAVES OTHER
FERRARIS
IN ITS WAKE

This racing boat gets its considerable go from
a mighty Ferrari V12 that was campaigned at
Le Mans and in the Carrera Panamericana

Words Gérald Guétat   **Photography** Henri Thibault

The driver activates the fuel pump and turns over the engine for a few seconds on the starter. Then a few pumps of the throttle to fill the carburettors, the magneto is set to position number three and a finger pushes the starter button again. This time it lights an inferno in 12 cylinders. The tachometer needle jerks round to 1300rpm then settles at 1200rpm. The water in the tank is heated slowly while oil pressure drops gradually from 100 to 50psi.

Briefly, the driver contemplates Alberto Ascari and Luigi Villoresi, who might have won the 1953 24 Hours of Le Mans behind this engine if not for a troublesome clutch – but today he's not sitting in their car, or any car, in fact. Meanwhile, the water temperature has risen to 60 degrees and the engine is shut off. Three minutes later it's fired up again and the driver engages the propeller shaft by means of a specially designed gimbal. He slips the clutch and the red racer starts to glide across Lake Como, leaving white foam behind it. The engine is hot, and now the driver can attempt take-off. Lift speed is achieved at the point where most boats have already reached their limit, but here the party has just begun …

THERE ARE THREE Ferrari-powered classic racing boats still in existence, but this is the only one equipped with an engine taken from a renowned competition car; the others have motors that were always intended for powerboats. This V12's racing career started at Le Mans in the year of the first World Sports Car Championship. Three 340 MM coupés were earmarked for entry, and one of them, chassis 0318AM, was upgraded with a reinforced chassis and a higher-capacity 375 engine – a 4494cc unit derived from Aurelio Lampredi's 1950/51 Formula 1 design. This particular engine was reported as having been prepared for the Indy 500 in 1952 with machined (rather than forged) con-rods.

Entrusted to the reigning Formula 1 champion Ascari and the vastly experienced Villoresi, the 375 MM recorded the fastest lap at Le Mans, and for much of the race it was locked in a battle for the lead with the Jaguar C-type of the eventual winners, Tony Rolt and Duncan Hamilton. But the big engine and the all-or-nothing approach of the drivers stressed the clutch to breaking point and, after 19 hours, the Ferrari was forced to retire, joining the disqualified chassis 0320AM back in the garage.

Anti-clockwise from top
Alberto Ascari poses with the #12 375 MM ahead of the 1953 24 Hours of Le Mans; the car retired with clutch failure, and its engine is today housed in this San Marco KD800 racing boat, seen being punted away from the dock by its owner, Dody Jost; in full flight on Lake Como.

*'LIFT SPEED
IS ACHIEVED
AT THE POINT
WHERE MOST
BOATS HAVE
ALREADY HIT
THEIR LIMIT'*

**1957 San Marco
Ferrari KD800**

Engine 4494cc V12, SOHC
per bank, three Weber 40IF4C
four-barrel carburettors
Power 340bhp @ 7000rpm
Transmission Propeller shaft
with manual attachment and
multi-disc clutch, twin-blade
propeller **Weight** 800kg
Top speed c140mph

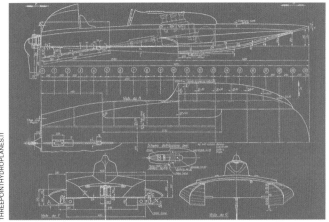

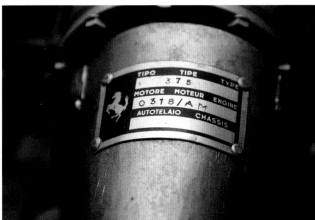

(For the curious, a mechanic had topped up the brake fluid of 0320AM earlier than permitted. Mike Hawthorn and Giuseppe Farina were no doubt less than amused.) Chassis 0322AM did manage to go the distance, and came home in fifth place, driven by the Marzotto brothers.

After Le Mans, the three cars were sent back to Pinin Farina to be modified for the rest of the season. The next race was the Spa 24 Hours, for which the other two cars were also fitted with 375 engines. Hawthorn and Farina claimed victory in 0322AM, but Ascari and Villoresi, this time driving 0320AM, suffered another clutch failure. Chassis 0318AM was also undone by mechanical problems, and its run of bad luck continued at the Carrera Panamericana – with tragic consequences.

All three sister cars were entered in the marathon race across Mexico, under the banner of Franco Cornacchia's Scuderia Guastalla. Antonio Stagnoli and Giuseppe Scotuzzi were given 0318AM, and as they were hurtling along a straight outside Juchitán de Zaragoza on the very first stage of the event, a tyre blew out. The car rolled and burst into flames. Scotuzzi died inside the car, and although Stagnoli was hauled free, he succumbed to his injuries in hospital the following day. Only the car's engine remained intact after the accident, and it was preserved at the garages of Scuderia Guastalla in Milan until it came to the attention of Guido Monzino.

MONZINO OWED HIS wealth to the chain of Standa stores established by his father, but his fame was entirely of his own making. He became a respected explorer and mountaineer, self-financing adventures to remote spots around the world and making several first ascents. In 1973 he led the first Italian expedition to climb Everest.

In pursuit of lower-altitude thrills, he ordered an 800kg-class racing boat from San Marco, the Milanese builder owned by champion boat racer Oscar Scarpa. The orphaned 375 engine, Monzino decided, would be the perfect powerplant for his new toy, and it was fitted to the boat in 1957 after being checked over by the race department at Maranello.

Hull number 069 was of the three-point type that dominated powerboat racing from the Second World War through to the mid-1970s. There are two wide sponsons at the front, while the rear ends with a narrow transom supporting the propeller and rudder mounts. At full speed, the hull is in contact with water at only three points, minimising friction between the hull and the water. The design actually works best on a lake that isn't perfectly flat: small ripples help to tear the hull away from the surface of the water from about 50mph, at which point the boat becomes a true hydroplane, running faster and faster.

Monzino's offices were in Milan, but he spent as much time as possible at one of the most beautiful houses on Lake Como, the Villa del Balbianello, which was used as a location for the 2006 James Bond film *Casino Royale*. His San Marco would be brought to his private dock from a nearby boatyard on request. He would climb, impeccably dressed, into the cockpit, cast off and speed towards the city of Como. Within 15 minutes, he would alight at the Yacht Club, where a Ferrari awaited to whisk him off to Milan. Now *that's* the way to commute.

He became an accomplished water pilot and took part in the Raid Pavia-Venezia, a long-distance race held on the Po (see panel overleaf), but by the late 1960s he was spending less time on the water, and indeed the San Marco had almost been abandoned when it was discovered by a student from the Fine Arts Academy of Milan in 1969. Monzino reluctantly accepted a meeting with the young man, an eccentric Austrian named Dody Jost, and a deal was done.

From top
A technical drawing of a typical three-point design, like the 375-powered KD800; the gearbox is replaced by a single gear directly engaged on the crankshaft; the engine-turned rudder mount is a little work of art; San Marco was the go-to boatbuilder for those with both a need for speed and plenty of cash.

Right
The V12 in all its glory. The cooling system had to be adapted for marine use: a dynamic scoop (it only works from about 25mph) beneath the boat collects cold water, which is warmed before reaching the engine.

When Jost took delivery of the boat, it was in need of expert attention; three-point hulls are delicate and one doesn't launch a Ferrari racing V12 onto the water without taking certain precautions. Jost went on to own the Nautilus hotel, which has its own private dock on Lake Como, and he kept the boat there for a few years before starting a full restoration.

The hull was sent to the respected Como boatyard Lucini, while the engine went to the Ferrari specialist Diena & Silingardi Sport Auto in Modena. The job took years to complete, but Jost's patience was amply rewarded. In 2012 the engine was given the official stamp of approval by Ferrari Classiche, and the following year the completed boat was exhibited at the Museo Enzo Ferrari in Modena.

Those who gawped at the boat when it was on display inevitably had one question: what on Earth is it like to drive? 'Well,' Jost begins, 'it's a delicate operation, because to go fast the hull must hover to avoid contact with the water except at the extremities of the lateral floats and the rear propeller. The engine torque is critical, because when starting up, the boat behaves like a mono water-skier. Fast engine response is essential to get the boat to lift out of the water. This is where the multi-disc clutch is crucial to provide maximum torque for lift-off. The hull of a racer is built to go fast; it's much more manoeuvrable when it's gliding across the surface of the water.'

There's a secret to steering this boat, too. 'The profile of the rudder is designed for high speeds and responds immediately to the slightest command from the wheel. The propeller is only half-immersed in water and you can hear its characteristic roar at full throttle – 7000rpm. The propeller rotates in a clockwise direction and tends to turn the boat to the right, which is why a small winglet is fixed under the left sponson to help stabilise the boat.

'Attacking a turn is very tricky because it requires the pilot to reduce speed but not by too much; that would cause the hull to sink back into the water, and bring the craft to a halt within a few metres. You really have to concentrate on what you're doing, but it's an exhilarating sensation – and the sound of the V12, of course, is fabulous.' *End*

ATTACKING THE RAID PAVIA-VENEZIA

The world's longest powerboat race

The Raid Pavia-Venezia represented a unique test when it was first run back in 1929, and indeed there are few inland powerboat races as challenging even today.

Competitors had to navigate some 400km of river, starting on the Ticino before joining the wild Po and then following canals to Venice – contending all the way with blind turns, floating debris, and shifting sandbanks hidden just below the surface of the water. The sandbanks were such a problem that regulations called for a riding 'mechanic' whose principal job was to dig the boat free if it became stuck.

It was inevitable that the Raid would appeal to the adventurous Guido Monzino, and he proved a useful racer. In 1958 he managed third place in the San Marco Ferrari, averaging 88.26km/h (54.72mph) and finishing in 4 hours 36 minutes.

END
of an
ERA

—— GREATEST RACES ——

1957 MILLE MIGLIA

A terrible accident meant that the 24th running of the Mille Miglia was also the last, but the race was notable, too, for the exploits of an unsung hero

Words Andrew Frankel   **Photography** Getty Images / Klemantaski Collection

Left and below
Enzo Ferrari with Piero Taruffi, who first drove for the Old Man when Enzo was running the Alfa GP team in the early 1930s; in the factory courtyard at Maranello, the cars are prepared for the 1957 Mille Miglia.

t is possible you have never heard of Piero Taruffi. As a Grand Prix driver he was merely good. He competed in just 18 World Championship Grands Prix, and reached the top step of the podium once, at the 1952 Swiss GP.

Peruse his results as a sports car racer and you'll note that he never finished at Le Mans, and while the record shows he won the 1956 Nürburgring 1000km for Maserati, a little further reading will tell you that he and co-driver Harry Schell were booted out of their 300S mid-race to be replaced by the quicker crew of Stirling Moss and Jean Behra, whose own 300S had suffered a suspension breakage.

In sports car racing outside his native Italy, Taruffi's greatest achievement was to win the Carrera Panamericana, a gruelling race the length of Mexico that was held five times between 1950 and 1954, before the dangers were finally acknowledged to be unacceptable. Taruffi won in '51, sharing a Ferrari 212 Inter with Luigi Chinetti. It was one of the less lethal years, with 'only' four fatalities.

From a statistical point of view, then, Taruffi's career doesn't bear comparison with those of his more famous contemporaries, but if they gave prizes for versatility and doggedness, Taruffi would be far better known today.

He began his competitive life on two wheels, not four. Born in 1906, he started riding at 17 and he won the European 500cc Championship for Norton in 1932. Five years later, he set a two-wheel Land Speed Record, becoming the first person to break 170mph on a motorcycle.

He came to car racing in 1930 at the age of 23, which was considered to be late even in those days, and he started as he meant to go on: with the Mille Miglia. The spectators who saw him waiting for the off in 1930 could surely not have imagined that this novice dressed in 'shepherd's plaid breeches' would, 27 years later, win the final edition of the world's most famous road race.

Yes, it really did take that long. He competed in the Mille Miglia 15 times, or 16 if you include the somewhat fraudulent 1940 event.

'TARUFFI THOUGHT HARD ABOUT RETIRING, BUT THE LURE OF ONE MORE SHOT AT THE MILLE MIGLIA WAS JUST TOO GREAT'

Above and right
Many other drivers had navigators, but Taruffi drove his 315 S, #535, alone, relying on his vast experience of the Mille Miglia course; the 1957 race became infamous for a tragic accident involving the 335 S of Alfonso de Portago, which careened off the road killing driver, navigator and ten spectators. A monument was erected in their memory, and you'll still see it today if you drive the SS 236 between Cerlongo and Guidizzolo.

That year, instead of a single lap of approximately 1000 miles from Brescia to Rome and back, the racers did nine laps around a 104-mile course.

Taruffi first encountered Enzo Ferrari in 1931 when his exploits on the Norton got him noticed by the man who was then running Alfa Romeo's racing team. The following year he drove a Scuderia Ferrari Alfa 8C in the Mille Miglia and failed to finish, but in 1933 he came third, again in a car run by Enzo, and at this point he must have felt his maiden win was just around the corner. In '34 he managed fifth, in '38 16th, but then nothing; he raced in the Mille Miglia nine more times through to 1956 and retired on every occasion.

Sometimes it was his fault. Twice he crashed – in a Lancia in 1954 and in a Maserati in 1956. More often, though, it was his machinery that let him down. Experience made him nervous of one particular eventuality whenever his car was provided by Ferrari. 'I began to wonder,' he wrote, 'whether the fast but bumpy and undulating Mille Miglia course might be extra hard on the Ferrari transmissions, making them the Achilles' heel of the cars from Maranello.'

At the end of 1955, and at 48 already an old man in racing terms, Taruffi fell out with Ferrari. To cut a long story short, Enzo had promised him a seat in the Venezuelan GP but failed to mention he'd be driving a slower car than his team-mates. An enraged Taruffi told Ferrari to give him a competitive car as per his contract, and when he received an evasive reply, he walked.

Life at Maserati in 1956 was no picnic, however, and Taruffi found the cars to be rather more rickety than the immaculately prepared Ferraris, weak gearboxes notwithstanding. So when Enzo offered a one-off drive in the 1957 Mille Miglia, Piero had some serious soul-searching to do.

He was worried about his age. In his last race for Maserati he was vying for the lead of the Giro di Sicilia with Olivier Gendebien when he slid off the road and ruined his chance of victory. Unable to rationalise the accident, he worried that he'd become reckless in his desperation to win, knowing his career was near its end. He thought hard about retiring.

And yet the lure of one more shot at the Mille Miglia was too great – so great, indeed, that he could not help himself even when it became clear that Peter Collins and Alfonso de Portago were to be given the latest-specification 335 S with a 4.1-litre V12, while he and Wolfgang von Trips would each have to make do with a 3.8-litre 315 S.

One more Mille Miglia, he told himself, and then he'd stop. To make sure, he promised his wife Isabella, too. Even Enzo told him to quit after the race, while assuring him that victory would be his. A quarter of a century after he'd

first raced for Ferrari, Taruffi was smart enough to know that Enzo had made the same prediction to all his drivers.

He did one reconnaissance lap, not because he needed reminding of the course, but to familiarise himself with his car. On the second day, instead of a mechanic he took Isabella, who was as unimpressed by the heat soak from the engine as she was stunned by the Ferrari's ability to spin its wheels at 95mph.

The day before the race there was the traditional press call in Maranello, where Taruffi looked at his eager young team-mates and saw the same enthusiasm he'd felt himself all those years ago. His memories of the day would later be coloured by sadness: one of the three young men had barely 24 hours to live, and the other two would both be dead less than five years later. All would meet their end while racing for Ferrari.

The following day Taruffi started at 5:35am, as indicated by the race number on his car. He was content: he might not have had the quickest Ferrari in the race, and he might not have been the quickest Ferrari driver in the race, but he knew the course in a way his hotshot team-mates never could. He reckoned local knowledge was worth five minutes over the distance.

De Portago was never a threat and Taruffi soon passed von Trips, who had started at 05:32, but Collins was gone. The Englishman was hurtling along on pace to break the course record set by Stirling Moss in 1955, his balls-to-the-wall approach evident in the streaks of burnt rubber that Taruffi found at the exit of each corner.

Wary of taxing his Ferrari's transmission, Taruffi drove more conservatively, staying in higher gears and reducing the number of shifts to a minimum, but at Rome, the halfway point of the race, he was told his policy had put him fully five minutes behind Collins. Taruffi recognised that caution would have to be thrown to the wind if he hoped to catch up. Now the Ferrari flew, literally at times, revs racing through the red as the car left the ground – but by Viterbo he'd made no inroads at all. All he'd gained was a strange noise from the transmission.

He could not beat Collins, that much was clear. But if he eased off he might just be able to nurse his Ferrari through to second, and second place on the Mille Miglia at the age of 50 would not be a bad way to sign off. Between Florence and Bologna, though, the noise got worse and Taruffi became thoroughly depressed, ruing his decision to chase the leader. More recklessness brought on by the desperation of an old man? It seemed that way.

The noise became so bad that he feared the transmission might seize and throw him into the scenery, so he decided to retire at Bologna.

'ISABELLA HAD TO TELL HER HUSBAND THREE TIMES THAT HE'D WON BEFORE HE BELIEVED HER'

But there he learned from Enzo himself that Collins's transmission was complaining, too. All thoughts of retirement vanished, but so did his gap to the chasing von Trips, who suddenly loomed large in the mirror. Once more the foot went down. In his hobbled car Taruffi couldn't keep the German ace at bay for long, but he didn't need to, because he still had the three-minute difference in their respective start times up his sleeve. Von Trips came past and Taruffi simply tried to cling to his exhausts.

In the end, Taruffi beat von Trips not just on elapsed time but on the road, too. At Piadena there was a blind left curve containing an enormous lay-by that almost doubled the width of the road. Taruffi, of course, knew it well. Von Trips did not. The German braked, the Italian kept his foot in and swept past, whereafter they stayed in formation for the short run to the finishing line.

Taruffi was somewhat surprised by the reception he was afforded – sure, he was an Italian driving a Ferrari and second place was a great result, but he'd not expected to be mobbed. Only when Isabella fought her way through the crowd to reach him did Taruffi learn that Collins had been forced to park up at Parma. She had to tell him three times that he'd won before he believed her.

Of course, this was a Mille Miglia with the most tragic of codas. About 18 miles from the

finish, something went wrong with de Portago's car. Some accounts say it was a tyre failure, others that an axle was to blame. Whatever the cause, the 335 S left the road and by the time it came to rest in a brook, 12 people were dead, including de Portago, his navigator Ed Nelson and five children in the crowd. For the race, too, it was an unsurvivable accident: three days later, the Italian government banned motor racing on public roads.

As for Piero Taruffi, he kept his promise, and while he'd later enjoy doing the odd regularity rally with Isabella, he retired from competitive

Above
With team-mate Wolfgang von Trips following him home, Taruffi takes the flag – still convinced he's in second behind Peter Collins, who has in fact retired.

motorsport that day. Peter Collins would die aged just 26 in the German Grand Prix the following year, Wolfgang von Trips at 33 in the 1961 Italian GP. Taruffi passed away in 1988 at the ripe old age of 81, and considering the fate of so many of his fellow racing drivers, that must be regarded as the greatest of all his achievements. *End*

IN-CAR COMMENTARY

Mark Hales and Martin Brundle share their experiences of driving Nick Mason's 250 GTO in the RAC TT race at Goodwood Revival

Words Mark Hales **Photography** Steve Havelock and John Colley

MARTIN BRUNDLE WAS coming out of Madgwick and up towards Fordwater when the thought suddenly dawned on him: 'I'm in a GTO, at Goodwood.' And then, with perfect timing, a Spitfire banked overhead to land. You have to pinch yourself sometimes in this job.

It was almost by chance that we were there at all. With a month to go, I wasn't lined up to do anything at the Revival. It has become such a high-profile show that people build cars specially for the weekend, so not only is an empty seat rare but, when it happens, Goodwood has celebs waiting, helmet and overalls at the ready. I've raced most years, but have never seen it as a right.

Then, joy of joys, Nick Mason decided he would enter his Ferrari 250 GTO after all. *Passion for Speed*, our opus about the cars Nick owns, was to be launched at the Revival and the GTO that forms an essential part of the narrative could hardly be left at home. Book-signing duties also provided Nick with the perfect excuse to sidestep the 'rather alarming prospect' of driving his priceless possession with me.

Last year, I had Marino Franchitti – Le Mans prototype driver; brother of Indycar champion Dario; and also Nick's son-in-law – as a partner, but this time his professional commitments in the US meant he couldn't do it, so I called Martin Brundle. It turned out he had been looking forward to a rare weekend at home, but on the other hand he'd never driven a GTO. Once a petrolhead… There was then the all-too-hurried task of getting the car ready for the race.

Nick's GTO, you see, is not a race car. That might sound a daft thing to say about a Ferrari that finished third at Le Mans in 1962, and second the year after, and which has competed somewhere most years since, but in the modern context it's true. Historic race cars today might look much the same as the ones in the black-and-white pictures, and most conform to the specifications set out in obsessive detail in the homologation papers, but they don't drive like they did. Most of them have been built from a bare chassis and are lower and stiffer, which changes the suspension geometry, and the brakes are usually better.

'I PROMISED THE CAR WOULD BE TESTED AT GOODWOOD AHEAD OF THE REVIVAL, WHICH IT WAS, BRIEFLY. MAYBE I FORGOT TO MENTION THAT THE SESSION WAS RAINED OFF...'

In most cases the engines have more power, too. American V8s and Jaguar sixes have been developed a great deal over the years, mainly because they are plentiful and relatively cheap – something that can't be said of the Italian exotics, which usually boasted more camshafts and spun to higher revs but are now even rarer than they were, not to mention more expensive.

Nick has owned his GTO since 1977 and the body has never been separated from the chassis. Apart from a few layers of paint and a bit of filler, the body is original and so are the chassis and the interior. And it still has its original seat, the black leather covering perfectly worn to brown by the slither of so many distinguished backsides. In the early years of the Revival, Nick and I raced the car several times, but it soon became clear that each year we had to drive harder to be further back in the results, and I couldn't help noticing that while I could keep most of them behind from Fordwater to Lavant, they would simply pull out and pass between there and Woodcote. Yes, I know all drivers say that, but it is definitely the case that, in comparison, the GTO has a little engine. Three litres is a lot less than the 4.7 of a Cobra, or even the Jaguar's 3.8, especially when it hasn't had the same development in recent years.

A few years ago, Nick decided that not only was the struggle a hopeless one, but it was a risky one as well. Additionally, if you can believe it, celebs apparently no longer wished to drive the car. Gerhard Berger, who shared the driving duties with Nick one year, is on record saying that, yes, he was willing to drive at Goodwood again, so long as they didn't 'give him a shit car.' He may have been talking in general terms of course. Happily, Nick eventually changed his mind.

The original engine (which has been with the car from day one) was removed and stored and another was assembled from parts but with the benefit of a few logical race tweaks. Apparently Graham Hill and co used to rev their GTOs to 9000rpm all the time, whereas we had stuck religiously to 7500. That is now 8000 and the difference is startling, at least three seconds round the lap, and another 15mph into Woodcote. The chassis and suspension, though, stayed exactly as they were.

I mentioned all this to Martin before the event and said that we were unlikely to win the race, but I promised the car would be tested at Goodwood ahead of the Revival, which it was, briefly. Maybe I forgot to mention that the session was rained off before Charlie, Tim, Ollie and I could really sign off on any of the changes to the set-up, or work through a pile of Dunlop L-sections until we found some that were all the same.

Maybe, too, we were given a false sense of security by the fact that the car was definitely quick. I could lap easily at last year's winning pace, a seductive detail that sometimes switches off the analytical part of a test driver's brain. Whatever, Martin's eyes were wide after Friday's qualifying. 'Two words,' he said, 'very, scary' – having nonetheless set a time good enough for sixth.

It was slightly depressing to note that the improvements recorded on our truncated test day moved us only one place further up the grid than we had managed last time. Last year's pace was exactly that: the E-type that had blitzed the pole last year in the hands of Bobby Rahal had repeated the time but was only fifth.

Martin wasn't happy with the Ferrari's brakes, so we decided to try some different pads for my track session on Saturday, only for me to find the rears locking like crazy every time I squeezed the brake pedal. That wasn't normal – it was akin to yanking on the handbrake just as you eased into the corner.

As for the rest, well, maybe I have become used to it. Even if I can see how someone looking through modern eyes might find the car scary, the fact is that's how they were – and that means that's how Nick's car is.

A FIRST-TIMER'S VIEW

Martin Brundle on his stint at the wheel

With the intense schedule of the F1 season and the other commitments I had in the the diary, I wasn't planning to drive at the Goodwood Revival. Then came an invitation to pilot Nick Mason's glorious Ferrari 250 GTO along with Mark Hales, and I quickly changed my mind.

A few years back I made a golden rule never to race anything I hadn't tested beforehand, but my travel schedule meant that went out the window. At some point I also agreed to drive an Austin A35 in the St Mary's trophy, so the 'rule' would be broken twice, and I'd have two rather different cars to drive.

I knew the 250 GTO to be very valuable but when I told friends what I was driving their first comment was always, 'Don't crash that, it's worth a fortune.' I had dinner in Monza with David Coulthard and the Franchitti brothers, Marino being Nick's son-in-law, and the banter was ferocious: 'So long as the chassis plate isn't bent you'll be OK!'

At a lovely dinner at Goodwood House, I found myself sharing a table with Nettie Mason, Nick's wife. I joked with her that I was thrashing round in her pension fund, although I suspect if I had rolled it into a ball they wouldn't go hungry!

The 250 GTO is beautiful and purposeful from every angle. The enormous tailpipes are the perfect advert for the V12. It's easy to feel overawed by it, even though I've driven some spectacular machinery in my career.

Sitting in the car for the first time it was immediately noticeable how big the steering wheel and gearlever and gate are. Everything seemed oversized even though there's not much space. I'm 5ft 7in tall so it was made to measure for me, although the gearlever was a stretch for my right arm. Mark is taller than me and has to fold himself in.

As I'm more used to carbonfibre survival cells, the single rollover bar above the driver's head seemed minimal. The main crash protection on the driver's side appeared to be my left shoulder and hip.

Leaving the assembly area for first qualifying session, I revelled in the power and sound as I negotiated my first ever 250 GTO corner at Madgwick. Just then a Spitfire flew through my field of vision, seemingly just over the bonnet. It doesn't get any better than that.

The car was nicely balanced, with a keen tendency to power oversteer in a controllable way. Being a pretty standard car, especially compared with some of the others in the Revival TT, it is reluctant to slow down from high speed and happily wags its tail in a disconcerting way as the barriers loom into view. The engine revs so easily that blipping needs care on downshifts.

I struggled with the gearlever initially but eventually set a time that put us sixth on the grid. It's a car you need to creep up on – understand its strengths and weaknesses, and then let flow. I found it's best to approach corners gently on throttle to settle the rear after heavy braking. I don't understand why they liked such big steering wheels back then

as it's not heavy at the helm and faster corrections would make life less stressful.

I started the race having not driven the car since Friday practice, but having practised and raced in the brilliant little Rae Davis A35 in the meantime. I felt rather unprepared, honestly, with a total time in the GTO of just 25 minutes to that point.

It leapt off the line only to end up hard on the brakes, boxed in with some slow starters. With a full tank of fuel, the car provided some nasty surprises in the first few corners on cool tyres.

Down Lavant for the first time I was getting mugged; it felt like I was carrying a 150mph Da Vinci and everybody was trying to steal it. Each time another driver stuck his nose up the inside I jumped out of the way. Being responsible for this important and valuable car was playing heavily on my mind.

I couldn't work out why the handling was so different, and why I was being passed on the straights. It turns out we were down on power for a simple reason, but it would remain that way for the whole race. The car still felt like a rocketship compared to the A35!

We pitted under a safety car and a well-rehearsed driver change worked beautifully, so that after an hour of racing Mark crossed the line in a very respectable fifth place. It could so easily have been a podium, but at least the car was in one piece.

I absolutely loved driving this beauty, but I didn't enjoy racing it wheel-to-wheel so much. Full respect to Nick and all the other owners who so generously let these cars race, with all the associated risks.

1962 Ferrari 250 GTO

Engine 2953cc V12, SOHC per bank, six Weber 38 DCN carburettors **Power** 300bhp @ 7500rpm
Torque 254lb ft @ 5400rpm **Transmission** Five-speed manual, rear-wheel drive **Steering** Worm and peg
Suspension Front: double wishbones, coil springs, telescopic dampers, anti-roll bar. Rear: live axle,
locating rods, Watt's linkage, semi-elliptic leaf springs, telescopic dampers **Brakes** Discs
Weight 900kg **0-60mph** 6.5sec (approx) **Top speed** 175mph (approx)

'I COULD IMMEDIATELY SEE THE PROBLEM.
THE ENGINE JUST WOULDN'T PULL ABOVE 6000RPM
AND THE REV-COUNTER WAS DANCING ABOUT'

Modern cars are much more planted, sit closer to the ground and, as much as possible, do all the work at the front. They let the driver brake hard and late, keep the weight on the nose, pin it down and aim for an apex with confidence.

A GT of the early '60s rode high and soft on its suspension so it was always floating. You sit the car down to add traction for the slow corners with judicious use of the accelerator, and take extra speed towards a fast corner like Fordwater, then ease the car in so that the roll sits the weight on the left pair of wheels and adds the grip you need to get through. Then you just balance it with the right foot against minimal tweaks of reverse lock. The problem is that, once you're committed, it's very difficult to change the line – and if you don't get the weight transfer right, the car will either wash out towards the grass, or the drift will become a tailslide that needs collecting pretty smartish.

As Brundle observed, you can't just send one up the inside and sort it out, and because you have to start braking from such a long way out, if whatever is up ahead wanders into your path, you are taking to the grass, or worse. It's then that the tens of millions of reasons for doing things a different way tend to flash into your mind.

In 1963 it was different. The car was just a tool, expendable like the engines, and that's why so many GTOs in the pictures have dents and scrapes. Surtees eventually said he didn't want to drive a GTO anymore because the potential to hit an Elite or an MGA was too great and he needed to concentrate on his Formula 1 duties. Back at the Revival, in an attempt to make sure we didn't hit another car of any description, I suggested some changes to the set-up and we put the best set of tyres on for the race, which Martin was to start.

He could have been forgiven for wondering what we had achieved at our test day, but his enthusiasm remained intact and details of the opposition's problems gleaned over supper on Friday night had been promptly sent via text, along with a suggested strategy to take advantage. And this from a man who drove in 158 Grands Prix.

The start of the race was as frantic as ever. We had agreed that a couple of places lost at the beginning was better than a shunt that would force us to retire, but there was no doubt that Martin had lost a couple of seconds a lap or more. I knew it couldn't be him and, since he hadn't pitted, my immediate concern was that my changes had screwed up the handling, or that maybe he had lost a gear. He had mentioned that it had popped out a couple of times during qualifying, after all.

Then it was my turn, and the pit stop practice that had provided so much entertainment to spectators paid off, the pace car came in and out at exactly the right time, and we gained four places. The good news, then, was that the balance of the car was back to scary-normal, and so were the brakes, but I could immediately see what the problem was. The engine just wouldn't pull above 6000rpm and the rev-counter was dancing about. Given that the rest of the needles were all where they were supposed to be, there was nothing to do but get on with it and maximise what we had.

The 'keep calm and carry on' approach netted us fifth in the end. It turned out that a plug lead had come off and we had done the entire race on 11 cylinders. It made the car feel exactly as it did before the engine was freshened. To be honest we felt we'd been robbed of an easy podium, but then again it's hard to be too disappointed with what is the car's best ever TT finish. And looking at the qualifying times turned by this year's hot rods, if the gods had offered us fifth on a plate before the race, we'd probably have taken it. Happily, we are due to start testing straight away in preparation for next year's event – so if it rains, we'll have time to go back again... **End**

Clockwise from left
Nick Mason's 250 GTO, a veteran of many
Goodwood Revivals, being hustled by Mark
Hales, who is pictured on the grid ahead of
the RAC TT; co-driver Martin Brundle making
the most of 11 cylinders, and executing a well
rehearsed changeover in the pits.

A DREAM COME TRUE

Nick Mason has been besotted with Ferraris since he was a boy, and thanks to the success of his band, Pink Floyd, he's been able to own many of Maranello's greatest hits

Portrait Ten Tenths

WHEN FATE DECREED that I could indulge in spending on sex and drugs, I frittered away my money on cars instead. It was my own fault: I demanded a dealer and got Maranello Concessionaires instead of 'Terry the Pill'.

My first Ferrari, not counting a 625A Dinky toy, was a 275 GTB/4. It looked a million dollars but cost a whole lot less – which mattered at a time when the world had only just begun to discover the appeal of psychedelic music. Of course, it never occurred to me to actually try the damned thing before buying it.

They say that the two best moments of owning a yacht are the day you buy it and the day you sell it, and by God the same was true of owning that 275. I can remember getting in it for the first time; the view from the cockpit was magnificent. But the car was a disaster. Its two greatest faults were a tendency to wet its plugs, and brakes that at low speed with reduced servo aid were worse than an Austin Chummy's.

I took the car to Maranello Concessionaires for some advice, and the well-spoken man who greeted me said he'd need to drive it to assess the problem. The brakes, he decided, were excellent – well of course they were, for the salesman was Mike Salmon and we never travelled at less than full revs. Mike clearly had no time for doodling around in traffic and couldn't imagine that I would, either.

Life with my 250 GTO, which I've owned since 1977, has been much happier. No car is perfect but the GTO comes close, and it fits into the family like a friendly labrador. We used it for my daughter's wedding, to the delight of the vicar. It's been very reliable, and I even did the school run in it one snowy day when nothing else would start.

The closest competitor to the GTO was my much-missed Daytona. It was a left-hand-drive example with two speedos that could be rapidly interchanged to allow for kph or mph. The fact that this also kept the mileage down was an added bonus! Although a Tarzan car to park, it was great on the open road. I did a lot of miles in it during a six-month period when I was working at a recording studio in France. I got through a lot of tyres and set some fairly politically incorrect times for Cannes to Le Mans, and Nice to Spa.

The F40 was the first Ferrari I bought new from the factory, and collecting it was a very special experience. Sadly I came along too late to meet Enzo, but it was unbelievably exciting to take my new car out of the factory gate and hammer up the autostrada. Rear vision was marginal (I later had some better rear screens moulded) but the design ethos was clearly that no-one would be overtaking you anyway. The fitted luggage still delights me: a thin disc of leather suitable for an extra-large pizza, and a wedge-shaped briefcase that was clearly designed for a chunk of Parmigiano-Reggiano.

I've had a couple of Dinos and still have great affection for the little Ferraris. I drove mine year-round, and I have an awful memory of hitting a patch of ice at the top of my street and sliding into the rear of another of my cars – which in turn went into the back of the nanny's car. I didn't have the nerve to fill in the insurer's accident claim form. I could just imagine the newspaper headlines: 'Rock drummer in three-car pile up.'

There was a brief flirtation with a 412. Auto everything and magnolia hide interior. Three-speed 'box and full four-seat capacity. I bought it with some crazed notion about practical family motoring, I think, and it was soon packed off to a dealer.

Practicality wasn't my main concern when I bought the Enzo, obviously, but it doesn't seem to have been considered at all by Ferrari. A quick time around Fiorano is important, sure, but Michael Schumacher should have taken the car to the shops to discover that the limited visibility at roundabouts creates altogether too much excitement. It really does go, though. I was amused when it was delivered to me, with 740 miles on the clock, that the chap felt it necessary to say, 'Still running in, Sir – please keep it below 200 miles an hour.' **End**

STAR QUALITY

This 275 NART Spyder is one of only ten made, and if that wasn't enough of a claim to fame, it also appeared with Steve McQueen in *The Thomas Crown Affair*

Words Marc Sonnery   **Photography** Jerry Wyszatycki

It's universally recognised as one of the most beautiful Ferraris of all time. The 275 NART Spyder was beautiful enough, indeed, to star in a classic Hollywood film, yet it had enough of the North American Racing Team spirit in its make-up to be at home on the track, too.

While the 275 GTB and four-cam 275 GTB/4 berlinettas delivered the wow factor with their iconic road-shark design by Pininfarina, the subsequent soft-top 275 GTS looked much more staid and left many dissatisfied. Not least Luigi Chinetti, Ferrari's Italian-born US importer and founder of the North American Racing Team. He'd been Enzo's ally from the start, and yearned to sell his clients a more appealing spyder, a worthy successor to the 250 California. Then, in 1965, he saw the first Nembo Spyder, made by Neri & Bonacini in Modena under the supervision of Tom Meade for client Sergio Braidi, who had wanted an open-top car with styling cues taken from the Series II 250 GTO.

The Nembo was hugely alluring, with its long, sensuous body and very steeply raked, 250 LM-sourced windshield. It was also uncannily similar to a Ferrari evocation from a Disney cartoon in which the car, driven by a fox rushing to see his date, snakes along the road's curves as if its chassis were articulated. The Nembo convinced Chinetti to ask Ferrari for permission to arrange for 25 of the 275 NART Spyder, as the model would become known.

His idea was simple: just remove the Berlinetta's top and the resulting car would be everything he wanted. Sergio Scaglietti's carrozzeria would prepare the modified coupés and Chinetti would pay for the series before offering the cars to his customers Stateside.

The roofless car looked spectacular, yet demand proved surprisingly low, and in the end only ten of the planned 25 examples were built. Of those ten, the car you see here – chassis 09437 – was the very first, and went on to become famous when it co-starred with Steve McQueen and Faye Dunaway in *The Thomas Crown Affair*. It received an alloy body, as did the second car. The rest were steel-bodied.

After it arrived in America in early 1967, 09437 was entered in the Sebring 12 Hours by Denise McCluggage, the respected motoring journalist and author who co-founded *Competition Press*, the publication that evolved to become *Autoweek*. She would co-drive with Marianne 'Pinkie' Rollo, born Wheatley and sometimes referred to by her first husband's name, Windridge. McCluggage mentioned many years later that Enzo Ferrari had teased Chinetti about the car's pale yellow colour: 'You make a taxi!' he'd said.

NART technician Roger Colson, a Frenchman who moved to the US about 60 years ago, picks up the tale: 'The car arrived in the winter of 1966-67 in Greenwich, Connecticut, at the NART headquarters. At Sebring you had to have a rollbar, so we fitted one along with a proper seatbelt, but I can recall no other modifications. We might have changed the gas tank, but that's it. We used the trunk floor as a pit board! I was the one holding it. It still says "IN" in chalk on the underside.'

The car took part under the banner of the Northern Vermont racing team, as distinct from Chinetti's North American Racing Team, because a fatal accident at the track the year before had implicated a NART entry. CITGO sponsored the car and, in a newsletter issued by the fuel company after the race, McCluggage is pictured showing her then-new book *Are You A Woman Driver?* to Mario Andretti, who had won the race with Bruce McLaren in a factory Ford GT40 MkIV. Astronaut Walter Schirra was among the celebrities seen with the team pre-race, and McCluggage was interviewed for television on the grid ahead of the Le Mans-style running start.

All six other Ferraris in the race broke down and retired, and one by one their crews came to help with the McCluggage/Rollo car. 'It was the only Ferrari that finished the 12 Hours that year,' says Colson. 'There was a Matra racing for the same fuel company, but I was alone on this car until the big guys started breaking down and everybody came to join me and help me finish the race! The car ran like a charm.'

Below from left
Period press cutting: Denise McCluggage and Pinkie Rollo brought the NART Spyder home second in class in its maiden race at Sebring, 1967; NART's Roger Colson – on the right in the previous picture! – with the boot-floor pit board; in action at Sebring; on the cover of *Road & Track*.

Pinkie Rollo was not as familiar to most as Denise McCluggage, whose writing had raised her profile. 'I had a very good impression of Pinkie,' Colson notes, 'especially her shifting as she passed by the pits; I recall her accuracy. She was very fast, not there for publicity.'

The ladies strung together 185 laps and finished 17th overall, second in the GT 5.0-litre class, right behind the Shelby GT 350 of the Los Caballos team, on the same lap. They beat several other all-female teams to claim a special trophy, including the pairing of Liane Engeman and the first woman to race in the Indy 500, Janet Guthrie.

Fame came calling for the car soon after the race, when Chinetti was approached by a film executive who had spotted the Ferrari and decided it would be a good prop for a major romance thriller to be filmed in Boston that spring. *The Thomas Crown Affair* was to be directed by Norman Jewison and would star Steve McQueen and silver-screen goddess Faye Dunaway, who was fresh off the hugely successful *Bonnie and Clyde*. McQueen cited her as the best actress he ever worked with; Dunaway, for her part, mentioned that *The Thomas Crown Affair* was her first time working with an out-and-out movie star.

Colson continues his story: 'After Sebring the car came back up to Chinetti's and the film company for *The Thomas Crown Affair* asked Mr Chinetti that we repaint the car in a specific colour: burgundy. That's the colour that the car was in for the film. I drove it up there to Boston to deliver it to the front desk of a hotel for the film production. I saw McQueen talking with people in a meeting in the lobby.'

Below and bottom
The Spyder appears just twice in *The Thomas Crown Affair*: at the polo match, with Dunaway sitting on its tonneau cover, and when McQueen spots the car parked on a Boston street.

'Steve McQueen obviously liked the car: he bought one of his own from Chinetti, chassis 10453 in Blu Sera'

In the film the Ferrari belongs to Vicki Anderson (Dunaway), an insurance investigator desperate to prove her hunch that Thomas Crown (McQueen), a wealthy businessman and playboy, is the man responsible for a major bank robbery. Having organised the fiendishly clever heist just for sport, Crown is baited by Anderson, who becomes ever more certain of his guilt. The car is first seen at a polo match, where she films him with an 8mm camera while sitting on the tonneau cover. Soon after, we see it parked outside an auction house in central Boston, where Crown recognises it before courting Anderson inside. And that's it! Just enough to leave you to dream of deleted driving scenes languishing in some archive.

The plot hinges on the brilliantly done romantic interplay between Crown and Anderson – the seducer used to getting what he wants and the not-so-innocent beauty. The film was made even more unforgettable by its score, written by Michel Legrand. He co-wrote the Oscar-winning *Windmills of Your Mind* with husband-and-wife team Alan and Marilyn Bergman, and that mesmerising song in particular helped cement *The Thomas Crown Affair* in the collective memory.

The film also stood out by making use of an innovative split-screen technique, showing different angles or scenes simultaneously. And it won a certain amount of notoriety for featuring the longest kiss in movie history, which took several days to shoot. Tough job, Steve.

Chad McQueen, son of Steve and actress Neile Adams, was seven years old at the time: 'Mom and I always came along to film locations. During production of the glider scene in *The Thomas Crown Affair*, dad took me for a ride on a Rickman Métisse motorcycle.'

Although Chad doesn't recall seeing the NART Spyder on set, his father obviously drove the car and liked it, as he bought one of his own from Chinetti by way of California agent Hollywood Sportscars – chassis 10453 in *Blu Sera*. 'Dad's car was gorgeous. At that age you remember odd details: he had the antenna top painted blue so that it wouldn't show when lowered. But he didn't have it long. One day he was driving to actor Stuart Whitman's place in Malibu and two sailors were distracted by a girl in a miniskirt. They rear-ended him, pushing him into the car in front. I never saw the car again.'

Neile Adams was less enchanted: 'To me a car is a car is a car; we had so many, and quite a few Ferraris over the years. In fact I bought him [Steve] one for his 34th birthday. But I'm afraid I can't tell the difference between one and another.'

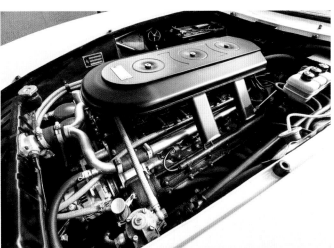

'On this fine day at Lime Rock, getting behind the wheel feels as surreal as a dance with Faye Dunaway'

1967 Ferrari 275 NART Spyder
Engine 3286cc V12, DOHC per bank, six Weber 40 DCN carburettors
Power 300bhp @ 8000rpm
Transmission Five-speed manual, rear-wheel drive
Steering Worm and roller
Suspension Front and rear: double wishbones, coil springs, telescopic dampers, anti-roll bar
Brakes Discs
Weight 1115kg
Top speed 155mph

When filming was over, Colson picked up the car from Boston. 'It kept that burgundy livery and in the September I had to take it to Lime Rock, right here where we are today, where I met the engineer from *Road & Track*. There were also two journalists from *The New York Times*. I took them around once each and then they took care of testing.' *Road & Track* called the Ferrari the most satisfying car in the world.

After that, the car was sold to Norm Silver of High Point, North Carolina, a collector who owned Ferraris including a 250 LM, a 400 Superamerica and a Daytona Spyder. Silver kept the car for 18 years, generously sharing the pleasure it brought him with any enthusiasts who crossed his path. In 1985 it was acquired by Dano Davis of Fort Lauderdale, Florida, and underwent its first full restoration, during which 09437 was returned to its original paint colour of *Giallo Solare*.

By 1996 it was owned by Bruce Lustman. A year later, 09437 was spotted in the back of the Colorado workshop of Mike Dopudja, who was taking care of it temporarily, by the visiting members of a car club. One young enthusiast, excited about seeing a true icon, began an impromptu presentation of the car to the group, then went to open the boot to show the chalk-marked 'pit board' floor, forgetting that he hadn't been given permission to do so. The workshop owner's wife gently but firmly said: 'We'll leave that in place now.' Yours truly had been told…

Lustman drove the car on the 1998 Colorado Grand, then sold it at Gooding & Company's Pebble Beach auction in 2005. It was bought by the current owner, a

major East Coast collector with a particular interest in Italian classics. In 2007, it was taken back to Maranello for Ferrari's 60th anniversary – its first visit home.

ON THIS FINE DAY at Lime Rock, getting behind the wheel of the car feels as surreal as a dance with Dunaway. As in an open Jaguar E-type, you sit high and feel somewhat exposed, and the simple, flat-floored cockpit and minimalist dashboard – reminders of the car's racing pedigree – goad you into action. So you oblige. The usual gated gearshift keeps your movements precise and deliberate, while the deliciously silken engine feels to have a more even power delivery than those of other four-cams I have driven.

Light pedal actions and steering, together with a body that is not excessive in size by today's standards, make the NART Spyder easy to command as it glides through pretty New England college towns. You feel you could drive it all day.

Then the road clears, with wide open pastures on either side. It's time to call upon the *cavalleria* to propel you towards the horizon while enjoying the engine's beastly roar – a soundtrack even Michel Legrand couldn't beat. It does not get any better than this. The mystique surrounding the NART Spyder is more than fully justified, which is a wonderful realisation after dreaming about the car since first seeing Dunaway regally sitting on hers all those years ago. *End*

Top and above
It's been resplendent again in its original *Giallo Solare* since the mid-1980s, following its colour-change to burgundy for *The Thomas Crown Affair*; the author at Lime Rock Park ahead of a long-awaited drive.

TOBY DAMMIT
Fantuzzi Spyder

For one of the three Edgar Allan Poe-inspired stories that make up the 1968 release *Spirits of the Dead*, director Federico Fellini cast Terence Stamp as Toby Dammit, an alcoholic actor heading for the skids who is given a brand-new Ferrari as part of his fee for making a movie in Rome. A lot of near-psychedelic satanic stuff follows, but the car is instrumental throughout. Gold in the film, and dubbed the Golden Ferrari, it was based on a 330 LMB, but the spectacular body is now worn by a 330 GT 2+2 (chassis 8733GT).

IL TIGRE
400 Superamerica

We tried to avoid foreign-language films here, particularly Italian ones – in which, as you can imagine, Ferraris crop up pretty frequently. But we made an exception for *Il Tigre*, released internationally as *The Tiger and The Pussycat*, simply because the 400 Superamerica is such a cool model to include. Cooler even than the 375 America used by Sophia Loren and Alan Ladd in *The Boy on the Dolphin*. It transpires that the omnipresent long-wheelbase 1963 Superamerica was the personal car of Vittorio Gassman, the star of the 1967 comedy about a middle-aged man who falls for the young girl (Ann-Margret, again) who broke his son's heart.

LIGHTS! CAMERA! TRACTION!

Ferraris have served as glamorous set dressing in many films besides *The Thomas Crown Affair*. Here are ten more movies featuring a scene-stealing Prancing Horse

Words James Elliott

GIVEN THE MARQUE'S prominence and desirability in the motoring world, Ferrari road cars have had a curiously muted movie career. This is partly explained by Ferrari's reluctance to get involved in such frivolous – nay, unnecessary – profile-raising pursuits, especially when, more often than not, you are expected to supply your precious metal for months on end, for free.

Of course there have been many Ferrari appearances, but rather than starring roles they have tended to be cameos, as was the case in *The Thomas Crown Affair* – total screen time a couple of minutes. Max. It is hard to think of too many occasions when a Ferrari came to own a film.

GOLDENEYE
F355 GTS

Ferrari must have been delighted that in this superb 1995 car chase down a mountain, an Aston Martin DB5 runs rings around its brand-new 180mph supercar. At the wheel of the targa-top F355 is the supposedly formidable assassin Xenia Onatopp, whose driving skills are shown up by a middle-aged Irishman mainly focused on seducing his passenger, a flustered MI6 evaluator named Caroline. At least working the Ferrari's clutch through the six-speed 'box (the paddleshift car was still a couple of years off) helped build Xenia's thigh strength, which would serve her well later in the film…

WEIRD SCIENCE
Mondial Cabriolet

We could have picked several other movies for the Mondial, the panorama-profiled four-seater being rather more popular with Hollywood than with the motoring press and the public. Most notable of the alternatives is the Al Pacino flick *Scent of a Woman*, in which Pacino's blind character Frank Slade drives the car like a lunatic around Brooklyn with his sidekick Charlie Simms acting as his eyes. It loses out for four reasons. First is that by the time *Scent of a Woman* was released in 1992, the Mondial could no longer get away with it like it could in the mid-1980s, when any Ferrari was the epitome of cool and sexy. Second, the plot is less plausible than a couple of kids creating the perfect woman on a PC. Third, *Weird Science* had a superb soundtrack. And fourth… Kelly LeBrock.

We're not talking about instances of a film being written about a specific car (think the Plymouth Fury in *Christine* or the Chevy Nova in *Deathproof*), but instances of a car becoming associated with a film to the point that it could easily be mentioned on the cast list with the stars. To the point that it will forever be remembered for its role. The filmic equivalent of never being able to mention the Reliant Scimitar without someone saying that Princess Anne had one, don't you know.

To avoid some of the most glaringly obvious examples, think Ann-Margret's Triumph TR3A and Elvis's Elva MkVI in *Viva Las Vegas* (see the race scenes for another example of Ferraris in cameo roles), Kowalski's Dodge Challenger in *Vanishing Point* or Grace Kelly's Sunbeam-Talbot Alpine in *To Catch a Thief*.

Our list omits two iconic films in which a Ferrari *apparently* starred. For decades, Claude Lelouch's morally questionable nine-minute motoring masterpiece *C'était un rendez-vous* was said to feature a 312P or 365 Boxer doing a daring dawn raid on Paris. A Ferrari – Lelouch's own 275 GTB – did provide the soundtrack, but to film a 312P speeding through the city would have taken more bravado than even Lelouch had. Rumours about both the car and the driver persisted long after the director had confessed the truth: it was not actor Jean-Louis Trintignant at the wheel, and it was not a Ferrari, nor a Matra as was also suggested by some. It was Lelouch himself, and the car was an urbane automatic Mercedes-Benz sedan, albeit a 450 SEL 6.9.

The most famous Ferrari in a movie, of course, was actually a Ford Windsor-powered replica of a 250 GT California Spyder SWB. One of the three so-called Modena GTs made for production was sold by Mecum in 2018 for $407,000. What *was* the name of that movie? Anyone? Anyone?

THE CANNONBALL RUN
308 GTS

Brock Yates' cross-continental dash inspired plenty of movies, including the David Carradine *Cannonball* and *Speedzone* as well as *The Gumball Rally*, but nothing in any of them is as deliciously hammy as Rat-Packers Dean Martin and Sammy Davis Jr playing a former racing driver and a conman while dressed as clergy and battling the JJ McClure (Burt Reynolds) and Captain Chaos (Dom DeLuise) ambulance across the United States. Obviously the presence of then-box office king Reynolds meant that the Dodge Tradesman (the same vehicle that Cannonball Run originator Yates had used with Hal Needham in the 1979 event) took top billing, but it's the Vegas veterans in the 308 who steal the show.

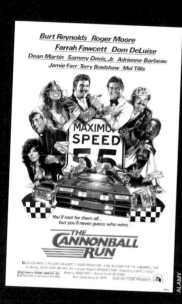

THE FLAMINGO KID
250 GT California Spyder

While the whole world bangs on about the *Ferris Bueller's Day Off* fake, it looks like a real Cal Spyder might have made an appearance in this less-well-known Matt Dillon vehicle from a year earlier. The bumperless car certainly looks the real deal and we have no evidence to the contrary. In fact – and we are happy to be corrected on this – if you freeze the action at the right spot, it looks as though both long-wheelbase and short-wheelbase Californias make an appearance masquerading as the same car. Continuity, hey?

GONE IN 60 SECONDS
195 Inter Berlinetta

We refer of course to Toby Halicki's 1974 original, which was enjoyable hokum, unlike the Nic Cage remake, which was unenjoyable hokum. We're also bending our own rules here because the Vignale-bodied 1951 195 (chassis 0115S) makes only a fleeting appearance – as brief as Parnelli Jones's – in what is admittedly a car-packed movie. However, this is a fabulously rare car (Vignale bodied only a dozen 195s) and one that looks quite unlike any other Ferrari of the period.

A STAR IS BORN
*365 GTS/4
Daytona Spyder*

Not just another Daytona Spyder but the very same cars (16467 and 14829) as in *The Gumball Rally* (see next page). The recent Lady Gaga and Bradley Cooper remake brings to mind the 1976 Kris Kristofferson and Barbra Streisand retread of the tale of two singers' mixed fortunes. The Ferrari – by 1976 the perfect ostentatious wheels for a rock star on the wane – appears regularly in the film and plays a key role in its denouement as Kristofferson's character John Norman Howard crashes and dies in 16467 (the already damaged car substituted for 14829 in the crash scene). The wrecked car was picked up by Luigi Chinetti (who else?) and reshelled by Michelloti as one of his wedge NART spyders.

THE GUMBALL RALLY
365 GTS/4 Daytona Spyder

It may be a just-for-laughs imitation of the Cannonball Run event (the movie came much later), but the cars and the action are real. Viewers are treated to an epic trans-America dice between a host of exotics, most notably a Cobra and a Daytona Spyder. The Daytona was 'played' by chassis 16467 and 14829; the former was damaged and the latter now resides in the Petersen Museum (see *A Star is Born*). What makes this film special for petrolheads is the way the cars are filmed, with the action snatching between wheel-to-wheel tussles, gearchange shots and redline close-ups – and the screaming, 20-cylinder soundtrack is marvellous. The camerawork makes perfect sense when you learn that the director, Chuck Bail, had previously worked as a stunt co-ordinator.

ALAMY

THE LOVE BUG
250 GT Tour de France

If having its F355 trounced by an Aston DB5 stung, a race-proven 1950s GT being humiliated by a VW Beetle must have really hurt Ferrari. In fact, the Tour de France (chassis 0585GT) is just one of two Ferraris that the possessed Herbie bests in this film's race sequence. The TdF was first sold to tycoon Tony Parravano – the one who disappeared in mysterious circumstances after a warrant was issued for his arrest in 1957 – and was later abandoned at the roadside in California. It is treated with rather more respect these days: it sold for $6.71m in 2012, and appeared at Salon Privé a couple of years ago. *End*

The company's association with Ferrari begins: an Allemano oil pressure gauge is fitted to the very first car to wear the Ferrari badge, the 125 S.

The company focuses on supplying precision instruments for use in industrial settings, but Allemano gauges are also found in the amazing Ferrari 156 F1.

1961

2010

Allemano builds a facility offering calibration services for all manner of precision measuring devices.

Fiat becomes the first automobile manufacturer to use Allemano gauges in its vehicles, starting with the Fiat 501 Torpedo. Other famous marques – Lancia, Alfa Romeo and Diatto – quickly follow suit. The pressure gauge installed in the 501 Torpedo provided the inspiration for the 1919 Collection of watches released a century later.

1947 Ferrari 125 S

1980s

Allemano conquers another sector, becoming a noted manufacturer of hyperbaric chambers and producing underwater instruments such as depth gauges.

1919

1947

1856

The company is founded by Giuseppe Allemano in the city of Turin, in north-west Italy, and initially operates in the field of heavy machinery, manufacturing steam-powered road rollers.

1950s

A key decade for the company, with its gauges found on board almost everything with an engine: aircraft, trains, ships, and racecars. Allemano pressure gauges are installed in the Ferrari D50 that carries Fangio to the Formula 1 World Championship title in 1956.

1929-1930s

Production increases with the manufacturing of extremely high-precision pressure gauges, thermometers and dynamometers.

2019

The 1919 Collection: Allemano produces a collection of timepieces that honour the company's long and distinguished history. Inspired by the pressure gauge fitted to the Fiat 501 Torpedo in 1919, the watches give classic car enthusiasts the chance to enjoy an Allemano instrument on their wrist.

Allemano 1919 Collection – Italian style, Swiss precision

Allemano

measure your time

CHRONO
emotions

LESS IS MORE

A smaller, lighter road car with half the cylinders – the Dino GT was revolutionary for Ferrari. **Andrew Frankel** compares the original 206 with the classic 246

Photography Tim Andrew

Even Ferrari, which in my highly partial view has made more beautiful cars than any other manufacturer, very rarely gets everything right. More than half a century has passed since the Dino 206 GT and Dino 246 GT were launched, and they remain the only strictly street Ferraris not to be saddled with a single imperfect angle.

We won't dwell on whether a Dino is actually a Ferrari or not. It was expedient for Enzo to put a little conceptual fresh air between his new baby and his V12 titans, but it was just a marketing ruse. Of course the Dinos were Ferraris, and indeed their influence is still seen in the 'junior' supercars made in Maranello today.

Our objective for this story, to drive and compare these two unimpeachably pretty cars, was complicated by the fact that just 153 examples of the 206 were built. Getting hold of one in representative running order is hard, even if you expand your trawl to Europe, where we searched for some time – before finding one almost under our noses.

When I arrived at Ferrari specialist Barkaways in Kent to see the car, I thought I knew how the 206 differed from the 246 it begat. Aluminium body instead of steel; 2-litre aluminium engine block with steel liners instead of 2.4 litres of cast iron; exposed filler cap; wheel spinners instead of nuts. Turns out I knew almost nothing at all.

Today, when a manufacturer decides a product needs a mid-life update, the brief is always the same: make it appear as different as possible while changing as little as you can. That's why items such as bumpers, light clusters and grilles are always being redesigned. They can dramatically alter a car's appearance, and at a fraction of the cost of re-tooling for bare-metal changes. Back in the late 1960s, Ferrari took a different view. When the time came to turn 206 into 246, the brief appears to have been: see how much you can change without anyone actually noticing.

The differences are so multitudinous that we've made a list (see page 93) so as not to delay us unduly here. But just for a start, did you know the cars are completely different sizes and that not a single panel from one could be fitted to the other? The 206 is shorter, particularly in the wheelbase, and lower, too.

Although it was the first road-going Dino, the 206 wasn't the first car to bear the name of Enzo's first son, who suffered from muscular dystrophy and died in 1956 aged just 24. Before his death, he and Vittorio Jano had been discussing plans for a new Formula 2 engine, and the unit that resulted was adapted for many racing cars, none more famous than the 246 Dino in which Mike Hawthorn won the 1958 Formula 1 Drivers' World Championship.

It looked fairly conventional with its four overhead camshafts and heads containing just two valves per cylinder, but could be told apart from other Ferrari V6s of the era by the 65-degree angle between its two banks of cylinders.

'I thought I knew how the 206 differed from the 246

that it begat. It turns out I knew almost nothing at all'

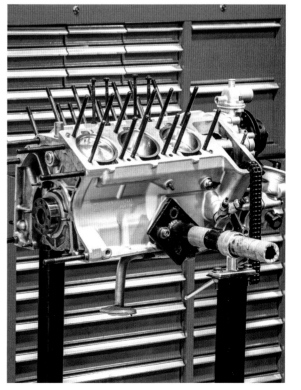

From left
At Barkaways, which currently has nine Dinos in its care, Ian Barkaway (left) talks the author through the key differences between the 206 and 246; the engine being rebuilt here is an all-aluminium 206 unit.

Key differences

Here we try to pin down the differences between a Dino 206 GT and a 246 GT. As with many things Ferrari in the 1960s and 1970s, this is not an exact science, with some early 246 GTs carrying over some or more of the features of the 206 GT.

Note: no Dino 206 GT or 246 GT left the factory with Ferrari badges. However, it is not entirely wrong for Dinos to wear them. UK importer Maranello Concessionaires equipped many 246s with both a Ferrari logo above the number plate and a prancing horse to one side.

	206 GT	246 GT
Length	4150mm	4235mm
Width	1700mm	1702mm
Height	1115mm	1143mm
Wheelbase	2280mm	2340mm
Weight	1140kg	1186kg
Engine cc	1987cc	2418cc
Bore x stroke	86mm x 57mm	92.5mm x 60mm
Carburettors	3 x Weber twin choke DCN14	3 x Weber twin choke DCNF
Compression ratio	9.3:1	9.0:1
Engine power	180bhp at 8000rpm	195bhp at 7600rpm
Engine torque	137lb ft at 6500rpm	166lb ft at 5500rpm
Specific output	90.6bhp per litre	80.6bhp per litre
Power to weight ratio	160bhp per ton	167bhp per ton
Body construction	All aluminium	Steel, with aluminium bonnet
Engine construction	All aluminium	Cast iron block, aluminium heads
Other differences	Exposed fuel filler	Concealed fuel filler
	Wheel spinners*	Wheel nuts (after Series 1)
	Six-slat engine cover	Seven-slat engine cover
	Pea-shooter exhausts	Standard exhausts
	Red line at 8000rpm	Red line at 7800rpm
	Full-length glovebox	Reduced-width glovebox
	Wooden steering wheel rim	Leather steering wheel rim
	Magnesium cam covers	Aluminium cam covers
	Exterior boot lock	Interior boot lock
	Floor-mounted ventilation controls	Dash-mounted ventilation controls
	Single oil filler	Twin oil fillers
	Small airbox	Standard airbox
	Numberplate light in bumpers**	Numberplate light in boot
	Door lock in side intake	Door lock below side intake
	Separate handbrake caliper	Integrated handbrake caliper
	Reversing lights below bumpers	Reversing lights below numberplate

*also seen in Series 1 246s

**also seen in Series 1&2 246s

'The issue with the 206 GT was that it just wasn't that quick, even for a car peculiarly marketed as "almost" a Ferrari'

Apparently this was Jano trying to ensure sufficient space within the vee for decent-sized carburettors, and as a consequence the crankpins had to be shifted by five degrees to ensure even firing impulses.

The first sign of a Dino road car came in early 1965 and, as ever with Ferrari, behind it all lay a racing agenda. The engine was needed to satisfy another new set of F2 rules – rules that also mandated the engine be based on a production motor. At least 500 units needed to be built for a design to qualify. Ferrari couldn't manufacture anywhere near that many, but Fiat certainly could, and it agreed to creat a sports car called the Fiat Dino and to use the new engine for that. One problem solved. The next was that Porsche was enjoying conspicuous commercial success with a new model called the 911, and Enzo wanted a piece of the action. He now had a production road car engine, but he needed a car to wrap around it.

The first concept was produced by Pininfarina in time for the 1965 Paris Motor Show, and bore the hallmarks of the design we love to this day – the voluptuous shape, the flying buttresses, the curved rear screen and the air intakes carved into the doors. The following year, the Dino Berlinetta GT concept shown at the Turin Motor Show captured in all but fine detail the look the Dino was to adopt, so when the production 206 GT was revealed in Turin in 1967, the biggest change was beneath the skin: the engine had been rotated by 90 degrees and mounted transversely behind the driver in the style pioneered by the Lamborghini Miura. It made the engine horribly difficult to work on but centralised its mass and, just as importantly, provided space for a surprisingly large boot.

It would be a flight of fantasy to say Dino Ferrari designed the car's engine, but it does have its origins in the V6 developed by Jano after his conversations with the young man. There's no mistaking its racing roots, either, thanks to the immensely oversquare dimensions. With an 86mm bore

Above
This is the early car, the 206 GT, with its wheel spinners and high-revving 2.0-litre all-aluminium V6.

and a stroke of just 57mm, it's no wonder it required 8000rpm on the dial before it would deliver peak power. How much power that was remains a matter of dispute: the same engine in the Fiat Dino was claimed to produce 160bhp, a stunning output for a 2.0-litre motor back then, but by the time it got into Ferrari's Dino it had gained an extra 20bhp… at least on paper.

Of course, the problem with small, short-stroke engines is that they lack torque and the 206 could summon no more than 137lb ft of it, way up at 6500rpm, necessitating that power ran to the rear wheels via a five-speed gearbox filled with ratios that were as short as they were close. It was all kept under control by a standard limited-slip differential, double unequal-length wishbones at each corner and vented disc brakes.

The issue with the 206 was that it just wasn't that quick, even for a car rather peculiarly marketed as 'almost' a Ferrari. In theory it would keep up with a standard 2.0-litre 911; I have to say I doubt it. Anyhow, the Porsche was not going to stand still, and Enzo realised that for the Dino to be a real success it needed to be faster on the road and cheaper to build – which is where the 246 GT came in. By enlarging the engine from 1987cc to 2418cc (though maintaining a very high bore/stroke ratio), Ferrari was not only able to up the power to a claimed 195bhp, but also to summon 166lb ft of torque fully 1000rpm lower down the rev-range.

Curiously, the 246 appears to have been only a little heavier than the 206 despite being physically larger, clad almost entirely in steel (the bonnet is aluminium), and fitted with a cast-iron engine block. Published weights for these cars vary greatly, but the most reliable I've seen suggest a 206 tips the scales at a not very sylph-like 1140kg, with the 246 just 46kg heavier. How can that be? I suspect the answer lies mainly in the massive steel spaceframe that, in design if not in precise dimensions, is common to both cars. Enzo's cars may not have had the greatest quality control, and they weren't made from the highest-quality steel, but he certainly made them strong.

I TAKE THE 246 GT FIRST. While I've never sat in a 206, I know its younger sibling well. Ian Barkaway, the founder of Barkaways, has provided an early 1970 model for the test. It's standard in every way except for the set of high-compression pistons he encourages owners to fit come rebuild time. 'Everything else – cams, valves, carbs – is to original specification,' he says, 'but the pistons just give it a bit of extra sharpness.'

Ignore the choke and prime the three Weber 40 DCNF carbs with a few pumps of throttle. Then churn the starter with just the lightest pressure on the pedal, and the engine growls into life. The only other V6 I've experienced that's as melodic as this was fitted to the original Honda NSX, but

the Dino's voice is richer, more layered, more interesting, if not quite so thrilling near the red line. I'd rather listen to it than any V8 engine Ferrari has made to date, and I prefer it to some of the V12s, too.

The spindly steel gearlever slots away and back, into first. The clutch is ridiculously heavy given how little work it must do, but it takes up the power smoothly and soon we are rolling. Barkaway has a secret gearbox mod that means you no longer have to avoid second gear when the oil is cold, though I've always enjoyed that particular Ferrari ritual.

We cruise at first, because you must take in the sights. I love it all – the rising curve of the wings, the grouping of the eight beautiful Veglia dials and the unimprovable perforated Momo wheel. Even the stuff I should hate, like the stupidly offset pedals and a driving position that favours long arms but short legs, all seems to add to the character of the car. The 911 achieved cult status as much for the things it did wrong as for those it did right, and the Dino's charm emanates from the same place.

Temperature needles start to heave themselves off their stops on this cold December day, warmth is percolating through the Koni dampers and I'm struck all over again by something I always forget: compared with modern supercars, a well set-up 246 rides like a limousine. These days so much secondary buzz is transmitted by tyres with liquorice sidewalls, but in the Dino, on its tall 205/70 VR14

Michelin XWX rubber, it's all damped out, leaving just pure feedback to reach your fingers. And because no-one ever thought a Nürburgring lap time relevant in a road car, the Dino is gently suspended on what would be considered comically soft springs today – yet it never feels sloppy.

Time to wind it up a little. Second gear, 3000rpm on the clock and let it go. The great surprise is that it doesn't feel slow at all. There's a solid surge right away, the growl becomes a snarl and you start thinking at once about how many revs you'll give yourself before pulling into third. I can remember as a kid gazing through the side window of a 246 at the tachometer and barely being able to believe that it would rev to 7800rpm. We won't be going there today, but close enough to feel the car in full flight.

You find yourself wanting to accelerate forever, simply to listen a little longer to that engine under full load. I wonder whether it would be more accurate to describe it as 'addictively exquisite' or 'exquisitely addictive' and decide on the latter. It is a sound of which no enthusiast could ever tire.

Sooner or later, however, you need to slow and climb back down through the gears. The brake pedal is a little mushy on this car, making heel-and-toeing difficult, but there's no snatch in the driveline, and the gearshift, while quite slow and heavy, is deliciously clean. There are corners ahead, and memories of 246 tests past come flooding back.

'The car, alive, on its toes, never stops talking to you; only an F40 is more communicative than this'

Above
The later 246 GT has a mostly steel body and a cast-iron block for its 2.4-litre engine, but the weight penalty is more than offset by extra power and torque.

The steering, I know, will weight up almost immediately, become flooded with feel long before the suspension is fully loaded, and guide the nose into the apex with unwavering accuracy. Even by Ferrari standards, the experience of guiding a 246 through a set of curves is special. The car, alive, on its toes, ready to change direction with zero notice, never stops talking to you; only an F40 is more communicative than this.

I know what a 246 does on the limit, too: it will choose to understeer a little, but this can be cancelled by the merest lift of the foot or transformed into equally gentle oversteer by the sudden reapplication of power. Unlike the other Ferraris of its era, the Dino is probably even stronger in the corners than down the straights.

What, then, will the lighter, smaller and presumably more nimble 206 be like in comparison? Well, I'll have to get into the thing first. Unlike the 246, it has a large wooden-rimmed wheel and, as with all 206s, it's on the left-hand side of the car. I just manage to thread my legs around it, only to discover I can barely select first gear. Headroom is somewhat tight, too. But I'm in, and not about to be deterred.

I don't know why, but while I knew it would be slower, I nevertheless expected the 206 to offer a sharper, more aggressive driving experience. I'd clocked the 8000rpm red line, seen its four pea-shooter exhausts and imagined its all-alloy engine to be even closer to a race motor. Not so. I wouldn't say it sounds completely different to the 246, but its voice is smaller, sweeter.

It feels a little odd at first, largely because what you notice are all the differences to the 246 – the still shorter gearing, the lighter steering and, most of all, the lack of power. Even with the high-compression pistons, while it is smooth and uncomplaining at low revs, there's very little shove. It starts to build from 4000rpm (just half way to the red-line, remember), and while I venture a little higher, I promised the owner I'd not stress his newly rebuilt motor. Were you to wang it around to 8000rpm, I suspect you'd see a different side to the car. The gears are close enough to keep the engine on the boil and I'd not worry about damaging it at all. Indeed, all the folklore says you're much more likely to harm a Dino engine – 206 or 246 – by treating it gently and never letting hot, thin oil properly circulate the top of the motor.

It feels a little more highly strung than the 246, less comfortable and slightly more antiquated to drive despite the fact that the two are separated by just a couple of years. But then Enzo was trying something completely new with the Dino, which wasn't just his first mid-engined road car, but also the first of an entirely new kind of Ferrari, so it's no wonder that the learning curve was steep at the start.

The 206, though, is also the purer of the two cars, with its ally body and block, slightly lighter weight, more compact dimensions and an engine even more keen to scream. If you want the clearest image of Enzo's vision of a road car worthy of his son's name, it's the one I'd advise you to drive, if you can ever find one. Otherwise, the 246 is better in every way – quicker yet more practical, more entertaining yet more comfortable. It's the finest production road car with fewer than 12 cylinders that Ferrari has ever built. And we'll go even further: to be on board, looking at the view over the bonnet, feeling the steering and hearing that inimitable V6 howling its song is one of the greatest pleasures ever afforded a motoring enthusiast. *End*

THANKS TO Ian Barkaway and the whole Barkaways team (barkaways.com), and to the owners of these two Dinos for allowing us to enjoy their wonderful cars.

'It's the finest production road car with fewer than 12 cylinders that Ferrari has ever built'

Nick Cartwright
Specialist Cars
Sales - Service - Restoration - Storage - Race & Track

A selection of recently restored Tipo 246 at Nick Cartwright Specialist Cars

Dino 246 GTS, 1973, Rosso Chairo / Nero

Dino 246 GTS, 1973, Blu Sera / Beige

Dino 246 GTS, 1972, Rosso Rubino / Nero

Dino 246 GT, 'Flares' 1973, Rosso Chairo / Nero

UK +(44) 01629 56999   www.nickcartwright.com   email: contact@nickcartwright.com

Brookfield Park, Tansley, Matlock, Derbyshire DE4 5ND

GREATEST RACES LE MANS

1965

Ferrari's final win at Le Mans was the most improbable in memory, and even now the events of the race remain cloaked in intrigue

Words Andrew Frankel **Photography** GP Library and Godwin-Stubbert Archive

The Le Mans 24 Hours is a fickle race; just ask the Toyota drivers whose car failed one lap from glory in 2016, gifting victory to Porsche. But I don't think there was ever a less likely winner than in 1965. Not only was the Ferrari that finished on top hopelessly uncompetitive relative to the quickest cars in the race, its drivers didn't even want to be there. What's more, there is evidence to suggest that there was an attempt to torpedo the car by none other than Enzo Ferrari. Yes, Ferrari's ninth win at Le Mans was far and away the strangest of the lot – not least because to this day it's unclear who did the driving.

The only thing anyone got right before the race began was that Ford or Ferrari would triumph, and the smart money was on the Americans. Ford had come to Le Mans the year before with brand new GT40s and the sole aim of beating Ferrari, only to see the cars retire one by one with mechanical issues, but that was very much a practice run. In 1965 Ford returned with six GT40s, four of them fitted with a 4.7-litre V8 – an engine bigger than any Ferrari had at its disposal. The other two looked more intimidating still: under the engine cover of each lurked a V8 displacing a whopping 7 litres. These formidable MkII cars would be piloted by Chris Amon, Phil Hill, Bruce McLaren and Ken Miles, first-rate racers all.

Ferrari did at least have a numerical advantage with ten prototypes entered, but just three were factory-run examples of its latest P2 sports racer and, of the seven privately entered cars, five were 250 LMs, which were only classed as prototypes because Ferrari had failed to homologate the LM as a replacement for the 250 GTO in the GT class. With single-cam 3.3-litre engines, they could not touch the purpose-built, 4-litre twin-cam P2 prototypes, let alone the GT40s.

Aside from one entire practice session being washed away by a freak rainstorm, the build-up to the race was entirely predictable. On pole sat the Amon/Hill Ford, a terrifying five seconds quicker than any other car. Next best was the P2 of John Surtees and Ludovico Scarfiotti, with a further three Fords rounding out the top five. At this stage few would have been paying attention to the LM entered by Ferrari's North America importer, languishing down in 11th place, a dozen seconds off the pace. If that sounds only a bit slow, consider that when multiplied over the distance of the race it equates to well over an hour of lost time.

The LM, too, was being pedalled by a couple of Formula 1 drivers, but these were not men of whom great things were expected; the career of the first was all but over, while that of the second had barely begun. We shall return to them shortly.

So the race began and to nobody's surprise the two 7-litre Fords just disappeared into the distance. But almost at once the Ford challenge started to unstitch itself, to the undisguised delight of the team from Maranello. The big Fords were phenomenally thirsty and their competitive advantage was blunted by the need to stop more often for fuel. Far more seriously, Ford had failed to anticipate the strain that the torque of the enormous engine would put on the transmission, and the 7-litre cars soon started to have gear selection issues. To make matters worse, the smaller-engined GT40s were struggling with various maladies, too.

After three hours Ferraris held the top five places; after seven hours not a single GT40 was still running. For Ford it was a total humiliation. For Ferrari's factory entries the race was already theirs to lose. And lose it they duly did.

'THE RACE BEGAN AND THE TWO 7-LITRE FORDS JUST DISAPPEARED INTO THE DISTANCE'

Clockwise from top right
The Ferrari P2s looked good basking in the sunshine before the start, but just one would survive the rigours of the race; Ford's GT40s fared even worse. The Müller/Bucknam car shown ran for only three hours and, after seven hours, all six GT40s were out; as retirements blew the race open, the 250 LM of Masten Gregory and Jochen Rindt suddenly became a contender.

It is easy to forget that Ferraris frequently won races – long-distance sports car races in particular – thanks to their durability rather than their raw speed. We tend to think of thoroughbred Italian competition cars as highly strung, temperamental machines, but Ferraris were generally strong and well prepared. As often as not, they won because they kept going when others faltered.

Not this time, though. One of the first to show signs of weakness was the unfancied 250 LM mentioned earlier. It wasn't even the North American Racing Team's lead entry; that was a single-cam 4.4-litre P2 crewed by Nino Vaccarella and the great Pedro Rodríguez. The LM came limping into the pits in the early evening with only six of its 12 cylinders firing. Jochen Rindt, who had not yet completed his first full season in F1, was waiting to take over the driving from Masten Gregory, the American known as the 'Kansas City Flash' in his 1950s pomp. The problem was nothing more than a dodgy condenser, but it took half an hour just to diagnose the fault, and by the time Rindt fired the LM back up the pitlane towards the Dunlop Bridge, they were absolutely nowhere.

By some accounts, neither Rindt nor Gregory wanted to be at Le Mans that weekend, least of all in a car with no chance of winning, and it seems those lost 30 minutes were the last straw. As they waited for the car to be fixed, it is said they agreed to drive flat-out because that would both alleviate their boredom and greatly increase the likelihood of an early night.

Meanwhile, far away at the sharp end of the race, other Ferraris started to fail. The two cars entered by the British Maranello Concessionaires team retired during the night, and then the factory effort came off the rails in a hurry. One after another the cars' brake discs, which had radial ventilation slots, started to crack and perish.

All three works cars along with the NART P2 were afflicted and the drivers were instructed to use the brakes as little as possible (tricky when the end of Mulsanne required braking from over 200mph to perhaps as little as 40mph), while all spare hands were sent off to find spares

or scavenge discs from retired cars. It was all to no avail. Drive a car faster than it cares to go in an attempt to make up lost time, while also using the transmission to brake in an attempt to spare the discs, and your race is very likely to end prematurely. Gearbox problems knocked out the two faster factory P2s, and engine failure did for the last of them. Of all the true prototypes in the race from Ford and Ferrari – 11 cars in total – just one finished, the NART P2 staggering home in seventh place and 28 laps behind the winners.

Now, with the 24 Hours only half done, a new race began, but not before a curious episode involving our hard-charging NART LM. All official records show its drivers to be Rindt and Gregory, and they are not wrong, but they may not be entirely right either. It has been claimed that when the famously short-sighted Gregory pitted unexpectedly in the small hours complaining of having trouble seeing in the dark, it was not Rindt who replaced him, but Ed Hugus. Why Rindt was unavailable is not clear; some accounts say he'd taken himself off for a sleep, not expecting to be needed. If Hugus did drive, he did well enough during his stint to keep the Ferrari in the hunt.

It was Hugus himself who made the claim, but he was by all accounts one of the good guys and a longtime NART driver. Moreover, in the endurance racing bible *Time and Two Seats*, János Wimpffen records Hugus' stint as fact. On the World Sports Racing Prototypes database, all three drivers are listed.

On the other hand, Doug Nye, probably the leading authority on Ferrari's racing history, considers the story 'total garbage – something the guy said many years later and then subsequently could not bring himself to retreat from'. Coco Chinetti, son of NART boss Luigi, felt similarly, but conceded he couldn't rule out Hugus's version of events: 'He may have driven the car but I find it highly unlikely.'

Whatever the truth, as the sun rose the NART LM found itself in second, and with Rindt back at the wheel it was travelling far faster than the privately entered yellow LM of Pierre Dumay and Gustave Gosselin.

'DRIVING FLAT-OUT, THEY DECIDED, WOULD BOTH ALLEVIATE THEIR BOREDOM AND INCREASE THE LIKELIHOOD OF AN EARLY NIGHT'

**Anti-clockwise
from top**
The yellow 250 LM of
Dumay and Gosselin
about to be passed
by the NART-run LM
of Gregory and Rindt;
a frightening blowout
on the Mulsanne
Straight eventually did
for the yellow car's
chances of victory.

The NART squad was still two laps down, of course, but Rindt and Gregory tore chunks out of the lead until it became apparent that, despite only 14 of the 51 starters still running, Le Mans had a proper race on its hands.

The intrigue was not over yet, however, for now was the time for the *éminence grise* to make his entrance. The problem was that Scuderia Ferrari was under contract to Dunlop, whose tyres were worn by the Dumay/Gosselin LM. The NART car was on Goodyears.

A Dunlop representative apparently paid a visit to Luigi Chinetti, who was not only the sole importer of Ferraris into the marque's most important market, but also a three-time Le Mans winner and the first person to win the 24 Hours in a Ferrari. According to Coco Chinetti in an interview with Doug Nye, his father was asked to let the Dumay/Gosselin LM win. Chinetti senior, always his own man, was having none of it – and even if he'd wanted to, it's doubtful he could have persuaded Rindt and Gregory to throw the race now, having flogged themselves through day and night.

For a while, it looked like the crowd would be treated to a grandstand finish. It seemed

'GOSSELIN DID INCREDIBLY WELL TO STOP HIS FERRARI FROM TURNING INTO A LOW-FLYING LIGHT AIRCRAFT'

Above
Members of the NART pit crew enjoy a ride on the victorious Ferrari at the end of a seriously gruelling 24 Hours. Of 51 starters, just 14 lasted the distance.

inevitable that the NART LM would take the lead before the flag, but it would then need a longer pit stop before the finish. Chinetti's lot were confident that Gregory and Rindt could pull it off, while their rivals were equally sure the NART challenge could be resisted.

We never got to find out who was right. Three hours before the flag, with the car flat-out at perhaps 190mph on the straight, a Dunlop on the Dumay/Gosselin LM let go. Gosselin did incredibly well to stop his Ferrari from turning into a low-flying light aircraft, but the exploding tyre caused massive damage to the rear of the car, and by the time it could be patched up all hope of victory had gone.

The record says that the NART LM finished the race five laps clear of the rest of the field, which suggests an easy day at the office. It was anything but. Had Masten Gregory and Jochen Rindt not decided to drive the LM right on the limit, no matter what the consequences, they'd never have been in a position to push the Dumay/Gosselin LM as hard as they did in the closing stages. Enzo might not have liked it all that much, but it was a very fine victory – and, of course, Ferrari's last at Le Mans to date. End

Mauro Forghieri

*Scuderia Ferrari won eight Formula 1 Constructors'
Championships and four Drivers' titles under this
brilliant engineer's direction. This is his story*

Words Massimo Delbò

DURING HIS LONG and glittering career as a racecar designer, Mauro Forghieri came to regard weight as his enemy. My enemy, today at least, will be space: Forghieri has many more stories to tell than I have pages to play with.

He was promoted to technical director of Ferrari in 1962 before he was even 27 years old and remained in charge for 25 years. In those days the technical director designed the entire car – engine and gearbox, suspension, aerodynamics, all of it. He was the last at Ferrari to do so.

'Back then,' he remembers, 'things were different. Sitting at my drawing board, I could picture the whole project in my head. Putting it down on paper was easy. Today, with the computer, your imagination is killed. You see only a piece of the whole.

'When I started at Ferrari in 1957 under Andrea Fraschetti, Ferraris – both racing and road cars – were very traditional with their tubular chassis and front engine. Mr Ferrari knew me because my father, Reclus, had worked in his shop since the early days in Modena, when they were making racing parts for Alfa Romeo.

'He gave me the assignment of designing the first concept for a chassis of a rear-engined car. To me it was a nonsense project. He picked me because I was the youngest, the least experienced, the least mentally caged.'

He wasn't regarded as the new boy for long. 'In 1959 I started working under Carlo Chiti, on "parts" of projects, not really knowing what they were for. Only later did I discover that they were for the first rear-engined racing car made in Maranello. Chiti never shared information with his people. Then, just after presenting the 250 GTO prototype, Giotto Bizzarrini left and I was assigned the first big problem to solve.

'The rear of the new car was very unbalanced, and Willie Mairesse went off the road. He swore it was not his fault. To understand what had happened, I made a couple of levers 2.5m long. Lifting the car with those, I saw that the whole rear axle was moving. The location was not firm enough.

'So we installed a Watt's linkage, and it worked perfectly. In April 1962, after Le Mans testing, Stirling Moss came to shake the hand of Willy Mairesse – the first man who could pass him on the outside.'

The 'Palace Revolt' of 1961 (see Romolo Tavoni's memories on page 20) resulted in higher-ups including Chiti and Bizzarrini being dismissed. 'This is how I became technical director,' Forghieri says, 'and I was made aware of it on the evening before the weekly meeting when everything happened. Nothing could be done. Mr Ferrari's decisions in such matters were always irrevocable.

'In 1961 we went on to win the Formula 1 Championship with Phil Hill. We had 25bhp more from our engine than the other competitors, but things changed the following season. Hill did not believe that we couldn't fix the situation, but the truth was that we had no clue. The engine was still my first love, but the English were moving forward with chassis development and aerodynamics. Innes Ireland, a gifted driver and engineer, gave me a perfect report on how the car was handling. We were in trouble.'

Forghieri soon managed to find a way forward. 'I spent days in Monza with my amazing team of designers, a crew better then with a pencil than a full team is with PCs today. We were waking up so early that the racetrack was still full of hares when we started practising. We learned a lot, we understood that we would need a monocoque, but for that we would need new tooling and new knowledge.

'In the meantime, with Walter Salvarani, I designed a normal frame made with rectangular tubes, to which we riveted the alloy body for the 156. It went faster in corners, but now the carburettors were suffering with the g-forces.'

GETTY IMAGES

GETTY IMAGES

Mauro Forghieri and Niki Lauda deep
in discussion at the 1974 French Grand
Prix at Dijon-Prenois; the engineer looks
down onto John Surtees and his Ferrari
158 at the Nürburgring in 1964, the year
that Surtees won the Formula 1 Drivers'
Championship by a single point.

One problem solved, then, but another created. 'So we hired the young engineer Michael May, a Swiss but born in Germany, from Bosch. He gave us knowledge of direct injection and we discovered how quick the reactions of the engine were with it. We ended up with a solution like Mercedes' and, after our first victory with Surtees at the Nürburgring, Mr Ferrari got a letter from the president of Mercedes-Benz. "We have to visit him," he said to me. That meant *I* had to go! Mr Ferrari handed me one of his watches, nothing special apart from the Ferrari-branded face.

'When I arrived, there were five Alfa Romeo Giulias parked up. I liked that. During the meeting, we spoke English and French, and I explained we'd use the solution only in racing and not for production cars. As soon as I gave him the watch, he lightened up. He was an avid collector!

'Several years on, I met him again, and he told me he still had his Ferrari watch. And about 30 years after that, I was working with Oral Engineering [Forghieri's own company] and consulting for several car manufacturers, including BMW for some F1 activities. One day, in Munich, I was introduced to a young gentleman, one of BMW's vice-presidents. We went on talking for a while and he told me, "I have a Ferrari watch. It was given to me by my father…"'

The sports-racers were Forghieri's priority in the run-up to Le Mans, but there were limits to what his small team could achieve. 'It was often me, stressed from the situation, who pointed out to Mr Ferrari: "We are 72 people, including you and your personal driver, and we have to take care of F1, F2, Can-Am, sports cars. We are not enough. We either need to double in size or we stop doing something."

'He didn't want to change, but he realised we were at a turning point. Ford and Porsche were obviously worried by us, and they began investing more heavily in their racing teams. We still won a hillclimb championship thanks to Ludovico Scarfiotti, and in doing so we became [Porsche team manager] Huschke von Hanstein's worst nightmare.

'Ludovico was killed in an accident in Germany in 1968. It happened about a year after we lost Lorenzo [Bandini, killed at the 1967 Monaco Grand Prix]. I suffered a lot during that time. I lost not only two great drivers but two wonderful friends, and it took me a while to recover.'

In 1969 Fiat bought 50% of Ferrari. The agreement was that Enzo would be left free to manage the racing department while Fiat would run production. But at the end of the 1973 season, Ferrari withdrew from all racing except Formula 1. 'Fiat's presence was minimal,' remembers Forghieri, 'and Mr Ferrari's decision was more a personal decision than an analysis. He just wanted to win more in Formula 1 and I totally agreed with him.

'Once Fiat arrived, we had no more financial problems, but still Mr Ferrari would check how the money was being spent. He always had a great respect for money. I think that's normal for somebody who had, for a long time, risked everything he had.'

ROBERTO BRANCOLINI

'WHEN BANDINI AND SCARFIOTTI DIED, I SUFFERED A LOT. THEY WERE WONDERFUL FRIENDS AS WELL AS GREAT DRIVERS'

Ferrari's financial success didn't just benefit Enzo. 'He transformed Maranello into one of the most renowned places in the world,' says Forghieri, 'but the relationship was not always easy. At the beginning the locals nicknamed him *Il matto*, "the crazy one", because he was driving and testing racing cars on normal roads. But he hired many people from Maranello, and soon the town realised that with Ferrari it had a bright future.

'Everybody who worked at the factory was supportive of the firm even though the salaries were never especially generous. At Fiat, and more so at Alfa Romeo, the money was better, but at Ferrari everyone was proud of their role within the company, from the blue-collar workers to the senior managers. We lived and breathed it.'

'WE "BORROWED" DISCS FROM THE CARS AND LEFT A NOTE PROMISING TO RETURN THEM AFTER THE RACE!'

ROBERTO BRANCOLINI

Even after Fiat's arrival on the scene, the ethos at Ferrari remained the same: it was always a racing team first, and its road cars – essentially lightly detuned versions of its racing cars – were a profitable by-product. More than any other manufacturer, Ferrari demonstrated how competition improves the breed.

'I remember when the 275 GTB was completed,' Forghieri says. 'From the first time I saw it and drove it, I was in love with that car. It was beautiful to look at, entertaining to drive and it fully respected Mr Ferrari's idea of a road car. He always said that it had to provoke the same emotions in the driver as a racing car.'

No single event improved the breed more than the 24 Hours of Le Mans, where cars are tested to the limit and where necessity has so often been the mother of invention. Forghieri has fond memories of the 1965 race, despite the fact that the factory team struggled. 'That year, Luigi Chinetti's North American Racing Team, heavily backed by us, was racing with P2s and 250 LMs. During the night we started having issues with the vented disc brakes: they were getting too cold along the Mulsanne Straight and then, when they suddenly heated up, they cracked. After losing the P2s, we had to come up with some way of making sure the NART 250 LM didn't suffer the same fate.

'It was Gaetano Florini who gave me the idea. Close by were the 275s of some customers. We sent a mechanic to dismantle their disc brakes, which had almost the same offsets as those on our cars. I told the mechanic to leave a note on the car, saying, "Sorry, the discs will be returned after the race!"

'We dealt with the small difference in dimensions by pairing a new brake pad with a used one. We won with the NART 250 LM, driven by Masten Gregory and Jochen

Rindt, and the happiest people of all were the owners from whom we "borrowed" the brakes. They felt that they had helped the team to win.'

Even Forghieri, of course, couldn't reign at Ferrari forever. He resigned in 1987 to work for Lamborghini, creating its V12 engine for the Formula 1 championship, and he then moved on to Bugatti during the Artioli years. In 1994 he founded his own engineering consultancy, where he is still active today. And yet Forghieri is still revered by so many as a Ferrari man above all else.

'This is natural,' he says, 'because what happened in Maranello during the 1960s, the '70s and the beginning of the '80s was so amazing that today it seems almost unreal.' With some prodding, he acknowledges his part in that success. 'Lots of talented people can design a good engine, a few less a good racing one. Fewer still can do so with a very limited budget. Almost none can do it under the sort of time constraints that were imposed at Ferrari, and under the direction of a man who gave *everything* in life to win car races. And only a crazy man, in the same circumstances, can design a whole racing car!'

Forghieri knew, though, that he couldn't maintain the pace indefinitely. 'I resigned because I felt that continuing under that pressure would kill me. The energy Mr Ferrari had was disappearing, too, and after almost four decades together I couldn't imagine staying on without him.

'When I told him my decision, he offered me a cheque. I thanked him, but said no. If I've been here all these years, I told him, it was not for the money, otherwise I'd have complained to you every month! I've been here because you allowed me to do what I really loved.

'He didn't get upset, but calmly replied that he agreed with me. He would have done the same, he said.' **End**

From left
Enzo Ferrari put huge pressure on Forghieri to deliver results, but the two men understood each other well; Forghieri at home – he maintains a better work-life balance these days!

DREAM BIG

The 1970 Ferrari Modulo concept is now a running reality.
Jethro Bovingdon speaks with the man who made it happen:
maverick collector and carmaker, Jim Glickenhaus

Studio photography Mark Dixon

Jim Glickenhaus gets it. He's a collector who loves to drive. He appreciates the artistry of great car design but has a passion for hard-nosed racing. He's steeped in the history of Ferrari but worries little about ruffling feathers at the factory. 'People kept telling me I was upsetting Ferrari,' he says when discussing his Enzo-based P4/5 project. 'Well, what are they gonna do? Come over here and kill me? No? Then I really don't give a sh**.'

Glickenhaus has a habit of doing the unexpected, from road-registering the ex-Bruce McLaren/Mark Donohue Ford GT40 Mk IV and clocking up over 50,000 miles in it since, to founding a car manufacturer and trying to win the Nürburgring 24 Hours against the likes of Audi, Porsche, BMW and Mercedes. Even old friends of Glickenhaus, though, must have been a little shocked when he drove onto the lawn at Pebble Beach in the Ferrari 512 S Modulo by Pininfarina. How was it? 'Oh, it drives great,' he says, like it's the most natural thing in the world.

Rewind to the Geneva show of 1970, and as the wildly futuristic Modulo sat under the bright lights amid a furore of shock, joy, confusion and awe, it did so with its 6.2-litre V12 empty of pistons. It didn't run then and it hadn't run since. Until Glickenhaus finally bought the car in 2014 and began gathering together the correct parts, scouring the world for bits of 12-cylinder engine, gearsets and countless other elusive components. For Glickenhaus, as for so many others, the Modulo was a dream. It's just that he had the means and the bloody-mindedness to bring this extraordinary concept to life.

Jim's father, Seth Glickenhaus, is a legend of Wall Street and established the investment management firm Glickenhaus & Co in 1961, building it into a billion-dollar fund. He died in 2016, aged 102, at which age he was still actively involved in the market. Jim worked in the family business, too, but not before forging a career in the film industry, writing, producing and directing a number of movies, including *The Exterminator* in 1980 and *The Protector* with Jackie Chan in 1985. However, cars and racing have been been his biggest passion since he was a boy, when he would clean and move cars for Luigi Chinetti, the legendary ex-racer and US importer of Ferraris.

'My relationship with Pininfarina meant I'd often wander through their museum,' he recalls. 'Against long odds I convinced Andrea [Andrea Pininfarina was running the company at the time; he would die in a tragic road accident in 2008] to sell me Dino Competizione [the unique 1967 prototype]. I always tried to get him to sell me Modulo, to which of course he said: "No, we could never sell Modulo."

'Every time I visited Pininfarina I'd try to get them to sell me Modulo, and they'd always say no'

Clockwise from right
The Modulo sprang from the imagination of designer Paolo Martin and made its public debut at 1970 Geneva show, painted black and orange; the rear 'window' is a steel panel punched with holes to reveal the (now working) Ferrari V12.

'And then, without going into it too deeply, there was a concern that perhaps the Italian government might seize the collection, as had happened with the Bertone collection. So I got a call and they said if I'd move quickly on it, I could get Modulo. I moved pretty quick.'

What next? Most people would clear a space in their living room (if you buy the Modulo you have a big living room), park it up and enjoy the view. Not Jim. 'When I got it, I immediately said: "Hey, I want to make it run."'

This would be no small undertaking. 'Modulo started as a 512 S race car. It was probably a spare chassis and never raced as a 512,' explains Glickenhaus. 'But it did race and run as a 612 S in Can-Am spec. They threw away the 512 body, made a 612, bored out the engine. It was chassis number 0864 as a 612, chassis 512S/27 as a 512.

'Ferrari, being a very frugal company, simply took the pistons out and the gears out of the gearbox when they gave the car to Pininfarina. And this young designer, Paolo Martin – who also did the Dino Competizione – roughed-up Modulo during the summer break at Pininfarina when nobody was around. When the bosses saw it, frankly, they hated the car. They were shocked by it and said: "We can't show this." Fortunately, they had a change of heart and it became a sensation.'

Once the parts were sourced to make the Modulo move under its own power, there were other problems to address. Like finding a way to make it steer without the wheels hitting the side spats. 'Actually we found the steering thing was more myth than reality,' Jim recalls. 'Ferrari had delivered the car on P4 wheels rather than 512S rims. They were too small and they'd used spacers to get the correct stance. Once we put on 512 wheels, modified the steering rack and removed the spacers, it all worked out.'

The final piece of the puzzle solved, Jim's team tested the car (now with the engine back in 512 S-spec, because he felt 550bhp at 8500rpm was enough for road use) before it rolled onto the lawns of Pebble Beach under its own steam. What a moment!

'I'm not going to do a ton of miles in this one,' he says. 'It'll get displayed sparingly, driven sparingly. I mean, I'm not sure I'd want to do over 60mph in the thing. Who knows, it might take off!' Besides which, Jim has other cars for when he wants to go a bit quicker. His aforementioned Enzo-based P4/5 by Pininfarina might look like a concept, too, but it was as much an engineering project as a styling exercise.

'We learnt some very strange things in the wind tunnel,' he notes. 'The Enzo had a lot of drag, it was very unbalanced front-to-rear, so we worked to ensure the P4/5 was better in every respect.'

Right and left
It lives! The Modulo moving under its own power at long last; the Pininfarina-styled, Enzo-based P4/5 caused tension with Ferrari initially, but was later given the factory's blessing.

NATHAN CRAIG

'The Enzo-based P4/5 might look like
a concept, too, but it was as much an
engineering project as a styling exercise'

For Pininfarina, the P4/5 represented an opportunity to demonstrate that it could still make traditionally beautiful cars. However, for Jim, the company's technical expertise was just as important. 'We took a lot of weight out of the car,' he continues, 'and we went to a wider wheel and replaced the Bridgestones with Michelins. The car turns in so much better on the track.'

It seems odd to be talking about racetrack performance of a one-off supercar commission, one that also debuted on the manicured lawns of Pebble Beach, back in 2006. And who would have guessed that an Enzo could be lighter to the tune of 270kg, was aerodynamically compromised and struggled with extreme track driving? 'Oh yeah, the Enzo had these weird hydraulic shock absorbers and if you went out on the track they overheated and it went into limp mode,' says Jim. These findings were corroborated by German race team Black Falcon, whose drivers tested the Enzo and a number of contemporary cars on the Nürburgring. Interestingly, the Enzo-based Maserati MC12 was found to be more durable and faster, too.

'We had to really beef-up that system to make it work,' he continues. 'The other thing about the Enzo was that it had two struts behind the rear window that were designed to stiffen the chassis, but they were mounted to a thin layer of carbonfibre and they were always cracking. So we took that out, we bulkheaded the car, we put new struts to the bulkhead, we put in an internal roll-cage… It's a much, much better car. When René Arnoux drove it, he was stunned by the improvement over the Enzo.'

I understand why people swoon over the Modulo, but for me the fact that the P4/5's central ethos is about hard road and track driving makes it even cooler. Of course, Ferrari wasn't so enamoured. It's hard to know what it was more upset about, the idea of a retro-inspired new Ferrari when Maranello was pushing forward-looking technology harder than ever, or simply that Pininfarina was hoovering up several million dollars that could have been flowing into Maranello instead of Cambiano, Turin.

Despite the initial mock-outrage, Luca di Montezemolo, then the president of Ferrari, quickly realised this was a special car, and it became an officially recognised model – the Ferrari P4/5 by Pininfarina. And funnily enough, Ferrari's own Special Projects department opened in 2007.

Jim's next move created even more friction with the factory. He took P4/5 racing. And because he never does anything by halves, he didn't quietly build a competition car and enter a no-name race somewhere in middle America. The P4/5 Competizione would race in the Nürburgring 24 Hours against all the big boys.

Sadly, the Enzo platform and the 6-litre V12 engine didn't survive the transition to the Competizione and the car was instead based on a Ferrari 430 Scuderia road car with plenty of 430 GT2 race car components fitted. The project was headed up by Paolo Garella, the former head of Special Projects at Pininfarina who had set up a new company to work in collaboration with Glickenhaus.

The Competizione debuted in 2011 and finished 39th after being slowed by several problems. In 2012, though, by which time a new KERS hybrid system had been fitted, the P4/5 Competizione M (Modificata)

'Who knew that an Enzo could be lighter by 270kg, was aerodynamically compromised and struggled with extreme track driving?'

Clockwise from right
Glickenhaus at the Nürburgring 24 Hours with the GT3 version of the SCG 003; and with the author, who was invited to drive the astonishing P4/5 Competizione (pictured here leading the P4/5 road car) in the 2016 event.

DAVE BURNETT

BRAD TRENT

finished 12th overall with drivers Nicola Larini, Fabrizio Giovanardi and Manuel Lauck sharing the workload. In typically cheeky Glickenhaus style, they also claimed a new lap record for a 'Ferrari-powered car' ahead of the 599 XX.

By now Jim's ambitions had grown, and with his passion for the Nürburgring heightened, he decided to go it alone: to develop a brand-new car from the ground up with LMP1-style aerodynamics that would conform to GT3 regulations. He wanted an overall win at the N24. Paolo Garella led the new project, which eventually resulted in the stunning, all-carbonfibre SCG 003. Scuderia Cameron Glickenhaus hasn't won the Nürburgring 24 Hours outright yet, but in 2017 it did capture pole position against the might of Audi, BMW, Mercedes and Porsche.

I had a little glimpse inside Jim's world in 2016, when I was kindly (and barely believably) invited to race the P4/5 Competizione M on its return to the Nürburgring 24 Hours. The pace of GT3 development meant we had no chance of winning – that objective would be left to the pair of SCG 003s also racing – but the old girl was still seriously quick and in with a chance of a very good result.

My memories of the car include its incredibly tight cockpit, shocking side and rear visibility (they agreed to fit rear-view cameras between first practice and qualifying, thankfully) and how my helmet would thwack into the roll cage hard enough over the bumpier sections to blur my vision. It was easy to drive, though. We couldn't hope to match the downforce of the GT3 cars, but it was dynamite in a straight line; the 4.3-litre V8 was an absolute screamer and it just felt so well balanced.

I really struggled with the old-school, lever-operated sequential 'box, and the KERS was intermittent at best, but going into the final qualifying session we were well placed in

22nd with a time of 8:44.449 thanks to Manuel Lauck's stellar lap.

The atmosphere among the guys running the SCG 003s was tense. They understood the level of investment required to get here and wanted a result. However, for me and Chris Harris, another of the drivers sharing the P4/5 C, everything was relaxed. Our aim was simply to get around cleanly and Jim was delighted to see his baby on track again. So, too, were the fans. They love this thing. Even better, after the final qualifying session, which the P4/5 C was going to sit out, I was going to jump in beside Jim and do a slow demo lap in his glorious, late-'60s Ferrari P3/4 chassis 0846 (whose provenance has itself been the cause of no little controversy, but that's another story for another day).

The sun was shining and everything seemed pretty good with the world as Jim and I waited at the gate to the track, GT3 cars howling past and the 4-litre V12 of the P3/4 warming up nicely just behind. Then my phone pinged with a message…

Unbeknown to the two of us, it had been decided that Lauck should do one more lap in the final qualifying session. It wasn't clear why. We weren't about to get ahead of the fastest GT3 cars and P22 seemed a bloody good result. Lauck duly destroyed the car in a huge shunt at Flugplatz, twisting the chassis and ending our chances of lining up on the grid.

We were all devastated. The remains of the car were being swept up and loaded onto a truck as Jim and I drove past on our demo run. It was a surreal moment. Jim simply looked at me and shook his head in disbelief. Of course it's back together now and road-registered in New York. Because, well, why not? Like I said, Jim Glickenhaus gets it. The next chapters in his story might not all revolve around Ferrari, but be sure to follow them. They're bound to be extraordinary. ◢

'The P4/5 was dynamite in a straight line; the 4.3-litre V8 was an absolute screamer and it just felt so well balanced'

Above, from left
The SCG 003, with power from a twin-turbo BMW V8, was Glickenhaus's first creation that owed nothing to a Ferrari donor; Glickenhaus at his garage with (from left) the ex-McLaren/Donohue Ford GT40 MkIV, a Ferrari P3/4, a P4/5, and the one-off Dino Competizione.

IF YOU DON'T ASK...

The Daytona was designed with motorways in mind,
but racers pestered Ferrari into building a track version.
We find out how the big GT handles in Competizione form

Words Sam Hancock **Photography** Paul Harmer

aytona was never the intended name for the car Ferrari still refers to as the 365 GTB/4; it was just a nickname, born of a famous 1-2-3 win at the 1967 24 Hours of Daytona, that stuck. And Maranello's somewhat reserved answer to Lamborghini's radically styled Miura was never intended to go racing, either.

It was conceived as a pure grand tourer, which meant it was not the most agile of Ferraris. It was, however, designed to inhale vast stretches of straight road, and this it did better than all of its peers – including the Miura. With a top speed of 174mph, the Daytona was the fastest road car in the world at the time of its launch in 1968. Surely not a bad foundation for a sports-racing car.

Caving to demand from its customer racing teams to take the fight to the armada of Porsches in the GT classes, Ferrari had its Assistenza Clienti department build 15 official 365 GTB/4 Competiziones between 1971 and 1973, in three series of five cars per year. Prior to this, there was a less-than-successful, alloy-bodied prototype created for Luigi Chinetti's North American Racing Team in 1969, but thereafter the model was made progressively lower, lighter and wider, and the elegant lines of the road car flared and bulged ever more imposingly as each series strutted off the production line.

While crude efforts were made to reduce aerodynamic lift (some experimented with chin spoilers and forward wheelarch 'fences'), the main focus was on handling and power. Homologation requirements demanding a partial return to steel body panels for the later-series cars catalysed extreme tuning of the famously reliable Gioacchino Colombo-designed 4.4-litre four-cam V12 engine, and by 1973 it was generating 104bhp more than its original 347.

Thanks to the prodigiously powerful engine and a weight-loss programme that took 300kg off the dry weight of the road car, the later Series III Competiziones were able to reach 60mph in 5.8 seconds and a top speed of 186mph, according to a test by *Road & Track*.

Racking up class wins at Le Mans in '72, '73 and '74, the Group 4 Daytona became so successful that a further eight privately commissioned conversions were completed in period, the factory having refused to extend production. Besides the five created by Chinetti, the car pictured here, chassis 16717, was the only other racing Daytona built by an authorised Ferrari importer, namely Garage Francorchamps of Brussels, Belgium. This earned it the factory's blessing and some assistance from Modena.

The donor car was delivered in 1973 to Jacques Swaters, the owner of Garage Francorchamps and the Ecurie Francorchamps racing team. It arrived sporting a deliciously 1970s *Maronne Metallizzato* (dark metallic brown) finish, and fitted with a leather interior and air conditioning. The car was soon stripped and resprayed in the traditional Ecurie Francorchamps colour of Belgian racing yellow, and the car has not been repainted since; the Luchard livery you see in these photographs is that applied by the team in 1975 for the car's successful appearance at Le Mans.

In what was to be the car's only competitive outing in period, it finished 12th overall, sixth in GT and first in the 3.0-5.0-litre sub-class. Drivers Hughes de Fierlant, Teddy Pilette and Jean-Claude Andruet were proud of the result, and rightly so – especially given the difficulties caused by the V12's prodigious thirst in the face of a new rule demanding at least 20 laps between stops. The drivers had to run the entire night using only fifth gear to reduce consumption, robbing them of their on-paper power advantage.

'A RULE DEMANDING AT LEAST 20 LAPS BETWEEN STOPS
FORCED THE DRIVERS OF THE THIRSTY DAYTONA TO
RUN THE ENTIRE NIGHT USING ONLY FIFTH GEAR'

1975 Ferrari 365 GTB/4 Competizione Group 4

Engine 4390cc V12, DOHC per bank, six Weber carburettors **Power** 451bhp @ 7500rpm
Torque 340lb ft @ 5500rpm **Transmission** Five-speed manual transaxle, rear-wheel drive
Steering Worm and roller **Suspension** Front and rear: unequal-length wishbones, coil springs,
telescopic dampers, anti-roll bar **Brakes** Vented steel discs **Weight** 1250kg (dry)
Top speed 186mph **0-60mph** 5.8sec

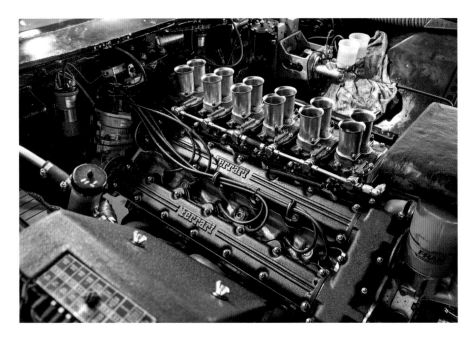

I strangely felt a few nerves while strapping in for the first time. Yet the Daytona, now prepared to perfection by Tim Samways, extends an immediate arm of friendship, with an easy clutch release to help you on your way. The moments before are less reassuring, however, between the monstrous growl from the front-mounted engine and a cumbersome clunk through a notchy dog-leg into first gear. 'A lot of power, a lot of weight and, I suspect, in a lap or three from now, very little brakes,' says the voice in my head.

Guilty on each count as it turns out, but thanks to the engineering efforts of Gaetano Florini and his team at the factory half a century ago, it's all entirely manageable. It's true the Daytona sits high and heavy like a bull elephant, but mass – if you have to carry it – can be used to your advantage. Sure, a little coaxing is required to adjust course from a considerable straight-ahead gallop, but once you're looking at an apex the vast body takes a set, loads up its outer tyres and generates a preternatural level of grip. From then on it's all about the throttle and, as you steer it on the loud pedal through the remainder of the corner, the Daytona exhibits a grace that many cars more petite in stature would struggle to match. The purist combination of mechanical grip, natural aspiration and 12 howling cylinders punching more power through the rear, treaded tyres than they can handle soon has me getting carried away. Which is where the trouble starts…

The Daytona is capable of astounding the driver once it's settled into a turn, but it's docile and lazy on the way in. Were the heavenly Race Resort Ascari an oval with just two corners, I dare say the car would be entirely at home here. Unfortunately there are 26 to navigate on every lap. Demand a change of direction too aggressively with any weight on the nose and the resulting pendulum effect will have you picking out your apex through the side windows. Do the same with the weight on the rear and the long bow will sit up like that of a boat, nonchalantly ignore your request and plough on with understeer.

The trick, I learn, is a deft combination of carrot and stick. Working with the car rather than against it, a pronounced, pre-emptive 'flick' on the steering just ahead of your desired turn-in gives the chassis warning of what's to come and starts the process of body roll. Then, when the time comes to actually turn in, the car is settled, poised and ready to go: cue main steering input. With a nod to Rob Wilson, the racing driver and legendary instructor, this approach is best described as 'little turn, big turn'.

Left
The cabin is a considerably less luxurious place to sit than that of a roadgoing Daytona, but the magnificent shriek of the 451bhp V12 more than makes up for it.

'PERFECTION IS BORING. CLASSIC FERRARIS ARE FABULOUS NOT IN SPITE OF THEIR FLAWS BUT BECAUSE OF THEM'

Gaining confidence, I get hungrier on the brakes. Small, vented steel discs and calipers more suited to road use nestle within all four of the Campagnolo rims and they're barely up to the job. And who can blame them? Slowing around 1300kg from speeds of up to 185mph is no mean feat. Ask too much of them and they overheat, and within a lap you're tapping up the pedal with your left foot between corners to regain pressure. Not ideal.

The solution, I discover, is again to give warning. Rolling smoothly off the throttle and onto the brake a little earlier than you'd like transfers weight from aft to front more progressively than 'fast feet'. This brings the car down a little flatter and spreads the task of deceleration more evenly across all four wheels rather than just the front ones. Responding well to this more considered approach, the initially alarming brake fade is minimised over the duration of a run.

Although it's slow to wake from the lower end of the rev range, the V12 just sings between 5500rpm and 8000rpm, reaching a beautiful harmonic so deafening at 7000rpm that you'd consider any hearing damage worthwhile. If only the straights were longer, because you just never want to lift!

And that's the point with the 365 GTB/4C: it is a vigorous sensory experience, but the experience is delivered in the most Italian of ways. Far from perfect, it is hot and heavy, the steering wheel presents itself at an angle more suited to an articulated lorry, taller drivers will bash their heads against the roof, the synchromesh 'box is slow and hates second gear – I could go on, but to do so would miss the point.

Perfection is boring. Ease is unrewarding. Classic Ferraris are fabulous not in spite of their flaws but in part because of them. And I can't think of a more satisfying all-rounder than a Group 4 Daytona, which represents the last generation of competition car that is truly usable on the road.

Oh, and it's rarer than a 250 GTO. ∎

THANKS TO Fiskens (*fiskens.com*) *for the car and for arranging the photoshoot at Ascari Race Resort (*ascari.net*). Sam Hancock is a professional racing driver, coach and historic car consultant. A former LMP2 Le Mans Series champion and Aston Martin works driver (GT and LMP1), Sam has raced at Le Mans seven times and competes regularly in historic events. (*samhancock.com*).*

A VISION

OF THE

FUTURE

Back in 1980, Pininfarina produced a remarkable
concept for a four-door Ferrari powered by a flat-12
engine. **Matt Zuchowski** went to Modena to meet it

Photography Konrad Skura

Few styling houses have such a long and distinguished history as Pininfarina, and none is more closely associated with Ferrari. So when the bosses at Pininfarina decided to build a concept car to mark their company's 50th birthday in 1980, it had to be something extraordinary, and it had to be a Ferrari. The Ferrari Pinin, named after Battista 'Pinin' Farina, was the result.

It was Sergio Pininfarina, Battista's son and by then the head of the company, who dreamed of creating a Ferrari-badged car to worry the luxury saloons of the day, which included the Aston Martin Lagonda, the Mercedes-Benz 450 SEL 6.9 and, notably, the third-generation Maserati Quattroporte, which had been penned by Pininfarina's arch-rival, Italdesign.

In the run-up to the 1980 Turin Motor Show, the city was abuzz with rumours that Pininfarina had prepared something special, but no-one knew what to expect. You'd certainly have got long odds on a four-door Ferrari, for there had been nothing like it in the marque's history, and Enzo's opposition to anything with more than two doors was well known. Imagine the intake of breath, then, when the curtain fell and an otherworldly Ferrari limousine was revealed. It was displayed alongside some of Pininfarina's most popular and familiar designs from the past – classic Alfas and Cisitalias – which made it appear even more shocking.

'There were rumours that Pininfarina had prepared something special, but no-one knew what to expect'

In 1980, the Pinin was revolutionary, not just because of the extra doors, but because of its extravagantly futuristic styling. It was by Diego Ottina (who would later contribute to the Testarossa and the 348) under the supervision of Leonardo Fioravanti. Looking at the Pinin, you can clearly see Fioravanti's hand in its angular lines, reminiscent of Ferrari's 2+2s of the time. The connection between the regular production models and the Pinin was more than skin deep. As with the recently introduced 400i, the Pinin had a transaxle transmission, with a five-speed manual gearbox mounted between the rear wheels. The new car was also surprisingly close in size to the 400i – only a couple of centimetres longer overall, and the differences in height and width were even less, but its low stance made it look radically different from mainstream early-'80s saloons.

It was far from being a remodelled 400i, though. Pininfarina redesigned sections of the chassis, and while the 400i used the evergreen V12 engine, the Pinin had the flat-12 found in the Berlinetta Boxer (and, later, the Testarossa) as well as in various competition cars. The Pinin was the only car in Ferrari history to have this engine installed in front of the driver.

In truth the flat-12's competition roots (it was initially conceived for Formula 1, where it powered the championship-winning 312T) didn't really fit with the idea of a limousine. It was favoured over the V12 because it allowed a far lower and more dramatic-looking bonnet line. Pininfarina didn't worry too much about noise or vibration for the simple reason that there were then no plans to move the Pinin beyond the mock-up stage, so the engine wasn't even connected to the transmission.

The Pinin's job was to showcase the studio's vision and flair, and this it did spectacularly well. The motoring world had rarely seen such a slick interpretation of the wedge motif in a 'three-box' body, while the details were a fascinating mix of old and new. Textbook GT proportions, two twin ANSA exhaust tips and a traditional egg-crate grille brought to mind Ferraris of yore, but here they were combined with other features that were genuinely forward-looking.

Many of these look fresh even today. The A- and B-pillars were black to create the visual effect of one uninterrupted strip of glass around the cabin. The five-spoke wheels looked like traditional Speedlines but were shaped to draw cooling air onto the brakes. And in pursuit of the lowest drag coefficient possible, the windows were bonded onto the body rather than mounted in the usual way, while the windscreen wipers were hidden behind the bonnet when not in use.

Variable-light lens technology had been mastered by Lucas just in time to allow the Pinin to have smaller and more streamlined headlights than its contemporaries, but it was the rear lights that stole the show. Made by Carello, these were tinted in the same silver hue

Above and below
The future, as predicted by designers of the 1980s: the instrument display is jet black until you fire the engine and it comes to life; passengers in the back got their own phone, trip computer and keyboard .

as the body and incorporated several layers of lenses that channelled the light in various ways to give it red, orange, or white colours. Many of the patents that made their debut on the Pinin later made their way onto better-known Pininfarina creations, including the Testarossa and the F512 M, the Cadillac Allanté, the Alfa Romeo 164 and the Peugeot 405.

Inside, traditional Connolly leather was used to clad cabin architecture that was utterly unlike that of any production Ferrari. The screen surrounding the analogue Veglia Borletti speedometer stayed perfectly black right up to the moment of starting the engine, when it burst into life with an array of function lights and auxiliary gauges. Most of the buttons and knobs had been moved to the central tunnel, while ventilation was by concealed slots that spanned the whole width of the cabin.

Rear passengers had individual power seats with a memory function, a hi-fi with personal headphones, a trip computer showing average speed and expected time of arrival, a keyboard, a telephone and individually controlled air-conditioning. And all this in the year that the Triumph Acclaim made its debut. To today's eyes, the Pinin's interior clearly belongs to the Duran Duran era, but it's impossible not to be impressed by the richness of the surroundings, and all that tech must have created a huge wow factor in 1980.

After its Turin debut, the car did the rounds of motor shows and visited the US, with the clear aim of exploring the sales potential for

'All the tech must have created a huge wow factor back in 1980'

such a car in the North American market – Ferrari's biggest at the time and the place where a four-door exotic had the best chance of succeeding. Back in Italy, the Pinin's fate was being determined behind the doors of Enzo's office. With him were his closest collaborators from the road car side of the business: Claudio Sguazzini and Vittorio Ghidella, delegated to Maranello by the Fiat emperor, Gianni Agnelli. Ultimately it was Ghidella's reluctance that terminated the project.

He had powerful arguments on his side, including the slow sales of the Pinin's strategic competitors and the huge costs that the development of a premium limousine would involve, especially for a company that had virtually no experience with cars of that type. As anyone who has sat in a Mondial or a BB 512i can tell you, at that time Ferrari's strengths did not lie in cabin build quality or refinement. It would have taken the company decades to meet the industry standards in these areas. Ghidella preferred to invest in city cars, such as the Panda and Uno, which were needed by Fiat at the time. His opinion didn't meet too much opposition; even Enzo wasn't sure about the challenge of putting the Pinin into production.

The red light from Ferrari meant Pininfarina had to put the Pinin on the shelf, and there it stayed until, in 1993, it caught the eye of Jacques Swaters, Ferrari's agent in Belgium and the founder of the Ecurie Francorchamps

racing team. He acquired the Pinin to join his collection, which included such rarities as a 288 GTO Evoluzione and a 250 GT California Spyder. As with all his cars, Swaters registered his new acquisition, even though it was still no more than a rolling sculpture. And so the Pinin was given its first registration plate – 20263 – on the isle of Guernsey in September 1999.

Nine years later, at the age of 82, Swaters decided to sell part of his collection at the *Leggenda e Passione* auction held by RM Auctions in Modena. There, lot 220, entitled '1980 Ferrari Pinin Prototipo' – still a non-running mock-up with the boxer engine loosely attached to the rest of the powertrain – fetched €176,000. The car found its new home not far from Modena, and one might have thought that the Pinin's story had come full circle. In fact, it was just the beginning of its new life.

The car had been bought by Gabriele Candrini, manager of the respected classic

Ferrari dealership Maranello Purosangue, whose premises lie just outside the famous Ferrari factory gate at Via Abetone Inferiore. Gabriele was determined to give the Pinin the life it had always deserved: that of a fully functional performance limousine.

Luckily he had the means and the connections to realise his dream, having at his disposal none other than Mauro Forghieri, the original architect of the flat-12 racing engine. The long-time technical director of Scuderia Ferrari (interviewed on page 108) was happy to be involved with the project, and many sleepless nights (and one large development budget) later he'd figured out how to help to Gabriele achieve his goal.

In order to bring the Pinin into life, the pair had to buy another Berlinetta Boxer engine and adapt it to its new chassis, merge it into a working unit with the gearbox and transaxle, design wiring and cooling systems and install a

'Light floods the vast glasshouse and the atmosphere inside is serene – while the car is stationary, at least...'

fuel tank. Finally, they decided to implement the self-levelling suspension that had been spoken about at the time of the car's debut.

Their efforts were rewarded in March 2010 and the Pinin was ready to move under its own power for the first time, three decades after its debut. Now fully operational, it was offered for sale with an attention-grabbing price of €1,000,000 but failed to find a buyer. Neither did it sell when it was offered by RM Auctions in London in 2011, despite being much more realistically guided at £500,000. And so it came back to Maranello Purosangue's headquarters, from where it was eventually bought by an American collector.

JUST BEFORE the Pinin departed Italy for its new home, we were given the chance to drive it on the Autodromo di Modena. A road test was never on the cards because the car hasn't been registered, but even on the track it quickly becomes apparent that Forghieri has managed to deliver a good measure of the luxury limousine experience promised by the Pinin's extravagant lines and sumptuous interior.

The cabin really is a good place to be: light floods the vast glasshouse, interrupted only by the thinnest of pillars, and when the car is stationary, the atmosphere inside is serene. The gentle suspension set-up ensures that the car flows beautifully across the tarmac, too – but for better and worse the tranquility is regularly shattered by a flat-12 Ferrari engine transmitting its 365bhp to the rear wheels with almost racecar-like ferocity.

You soon learn to enjoy the juxtaposition of refinement and raucousness – it certainly gives the car a unique character – but there are some other issues that would make driving the Pinin on the road tricky at best.

It's still a prototype, after all, and the space taken up by the engine and its peripherals mean the steering system has a limited ability to turn left. What's more, the driver would need to be constantly on the look-out for any sudden bumps or dips because of the minimal ground clearance – the consequence of the engine being pushed down by the low bonnet.

All these issues would, of course, have been addressed had the Pinin project progressed. And after spending a day with this car you can't help but think of it as of a missed opportunity. From behind the steering wheel of the Pinin it's not difficult to imagine an alternative history of Ferrari with a four-door Lagonda rival coming off the production line in Maranello. Against all the odds, a Ferrari limousine might just have worked – and while we have no indication of Ferrari's intentions for the 2022 SUV currently known as the Purosangue, it's quite possible we won't have to wait much longer for another exception to Enzo's two-door rule. *End*

FURLONGER
· SPECIALIST CARS ·

DEDICATION, PASSION, ENTHUSIASM AND EXPERIENCE

Extensive Range of Cars for Sale

Furlonger have sourced, purchased, supplied, serviced and restored some of the most collectible vehicles in the world. Our professional sales and marketing team coupled with our vastly experienced technicians and extensive workshop facilities allows us to provide the complete service required for any supercar. We also offer a range of storage options via our secure local facility. Whether your classic Ferrari or Lamborghini requires a major overhaul, your McLaren requires a service or secure storage, Furlonger are equipped and completely prepared to do so.

SERVICING DEPARTMENT

Ferrari
With over 100 years combined experience, we can look after every aspect of both your modern and classic Ferrari.

Lamborghini
Specialising in Lamborghinis built from the 1960's to the present day, we can cater for all your cars needs and pride ourselves as V12 experts.

McLaren
Since 2016 we have taken on multiple McLarens for comprehensive maintenance and routine servicing.

Bugatti EB110
With extensive experience and the support of the world's leading parts suppliers, we can provide comprehensive maintenance on all EB110s.

Chart Enterprise Park, Dencora Way, Ashford, Kent, United Kingdom TN23 4FL. Tel: +44 (0) 1233 646328
www.simonfurlonger.co.uk

THE SECOND COMING

Back in 1995, *Car* magazine drove to the Sahara Desert in a brand-new F512 M. Now **Harry Metcalfe** repeats the journey in his own Testarossa – without the back-up crew

Photography Justin Leighton

141

Finding the main route out of Tangier is proving to be a nightmare. The guidebook I bought weeks ago said to avoid Tangier City and enter Morocco via Tangier Med – but I only got around to reading it just before we disembarked from the ferry. The fact that I'm in a low-flying Ferrari without any form of GPS navigation isn't helping. Decent tarmac seems to be scarce in Tangier and there are no roadsigns to guide visitors out of its confusing maze of bustling streets.

We sweep blindly round a corner, locked in a scrum with battered cars as if in a banger race, and it's about to get worse: ahead the road is blocked, forcing all traffic through an Oil Libya fuel station that was never designed to have the main road running through it. It's a chaotic scene, the poor fuel attendants doing their best to dodge the two-way traffic. The biggest issue, though, is the difference in height between the concrete forecourt and the temporary road surface beyond – about a foot. I refuse to commit the Testarossa to a chassis-damaging drop, and behind me a queue of irritable taxi drivers (in disturbingly distressed Mercedes dating mainly from the 1970s) is quickly forming. They can't understand what the problem is, and think the Testarossa must be some sort of joke because it's only got two seats and has no space for livestock. It's fair to say that this is not the welcome I was hoping for.

The reason I'm here and subjecting the Testarossa to this torture is a feature written by Richard Bremner back in 1995, for *Car* magazine. Richard drove a then-new F512 M all the way from Maranello to the Sahara Desert, and his account of the journey was one of the best drive stories I'd ever read. Since I now own a Testarossa and love doing long road trips, I thought it would be fun to attempt something similar myself – and until we reached Tangier it had all been going swimmingly.

WE'D SET OFF two days earlier on an overnight ferry to Spain, leaving Portsmouth around noon and arriving in Santander at 3pm the following day. From there it was just a 640-mile dash down to Tarifa in the very south of Spain to catch the high-speed ferry to Morocco.

The A6 is the main route out of Santander, and we left the outer suburbs to head for the hills, where the Testarossa settled into an easy canter as we climbed away from the rugged northern coastline. The mid-February sun felt quite strong through the windscreen but, ominously, patches of snow started to appear in shaded hollows by the side of the road. Snow isn't unusual in this part of Spain at this time of year, and had we set off only a week earlier this road would barely have been passable, such was the covering the region received.

Inside the car, I was congratulating myself for having recently fitted a 50mm extension just behind the steering wheel to bring it closer to the driver; it makes a much bigger difference in terms of comfort than you'd ever imagine. I was beginning to recognise, too, that the Testarossa's stylised seats are surprisingly accommodating for long journeys, even though adjustments are relatively few. All I'm missing now is a decent rest for my left foot during long passages of motorway cruising.

Another early surprise was the distance that the Testarossa can cover between fill-ups. The fuel tank is vast at 118 litres (25.2 imperial gallons), and when you're pottering along a motorway at close(ish) to the national speed limit, the mpg can soon climb into the low 20s, meaning the reserve light only starts winking at you after 400 miles or so have passed. The icing on the cake at the time of our visit was that unleaded in Spain cost the equivalent of 90p per litre and, with Spanish policing noticeable only by its absence, we were soon barrelling across the country, our speed really only tempered by our tolerance for wind noise.

MINERAUX FOSSILES D'ATLAS

DRIVING IN MOROCCO

Choose your ferry wisely,
take plenty of cash, and
absolutely do not speed!

Stating the obvious, Morocco is
a very long way away from the UK.
We shortened the distance travelled
by taking an overnight ferry from
Portsmouth to Santander.

Choose your crossing between
Spain and Morocco with care. We
made the 'mistake' of booking a
crossing that delivers you at Tangier
City, which proved a nightmare to
navigate out of. The best ferry is the
service operating between Algeciras
and 'Port Tangier Mediterranee'
further up the coast, which links
directly on to the A4 motorway.

On the ferry across, you need to
get your passport stamped before
entering Morocco and then you have
to clear customs, who will search
your car and inspect the registration
papers and insurance documents
in minute detail. Allow at least an
hour to clear.

Next, make sure you have plenty
of dirhams on you, because you have
to pay with cash almost everywhere.
Motorway tolls, fuel stations, even
hotels in the sticks only accept cash,
and finding an ATM isn't easy.

As for driving in Morocco, I've
never visited anywhere with more
speed traps, so stick to the speed
limit. If you get stopped (and you
will), the police will want paying in
cash, or your car will be confiscated.

Driving at night is best avoided
because it's so dangerous.
Remember, too, that 'sports cars'
are rare in Morocco, which makes
finding replacement tyres next to
impossible, and any breakdown
is serious because there's no
national rescue service, either.
Good luck!

We'd booked a motel just north of Seville for our first stop and awoke the next day to find the Testarossa surrounded by serious off-roaders, all heading to Morocco as support vehicles for the annual 4L Trophy. The event sees more than 1000 Renault 4s being tested to the limit over 1500km of trails in the desert, and there was disbelief among the 4x4 drivers when I revealed we were heading there, too. They kindly promised to help out if we got into difficulty, which was very reassuring; I had discovered a few weeks earlier that there's no rescue service on offer from the likes of the RAC and the AA if you venture into Morocco. Another unwelcome discovery was that UK-issued insurance policies generally only cover driving in Europe, so cover for Morocco needs to be arranged separately and isn't automatically available… especially if you're taking a classic Ferrari into the Sahara.

We reached Tarifa in good time, found the right queue for the ferry, clambered out and stretched our legs. Mrs Metcalfe was very grateful that there was not a breath of wind, meaning there was every chance of a smooth crossing to Morocco. I was more chuffed by the way the Testarossa had demolished the previous 640 miles without any issues. My only slight concern was what came next because, in typical bloke fashion, I chose which crossing to take purely on how cool the ferry looked in pictures. So we were queuing for FRS's *Tarifa Jet*, a catamaran packing a monstrous 38,500hp, giving it a cruising speed of 42 knots (48mph). It gets you to Morocco in a mere 35 minutes. However, the guidebook I read on board warned its readers not to book this particular crossing because *Tarifa Jet* docks in Tangier City, which is not tourist friendly at all. As we were to discover when we drove out of customs and got caught up in the mayhem at the petrol station.

I'M STILL REFUSING to drive over the huge concrete step blocking our route ahead. There's nothing for it but to get the cars behind to back up, allowing us to turn around and then look for another route out of Tangier's inner-city mayhem. With only the compass on my iPhone to guide us in the right direction, we finally discover a motorway sign. A sense of calm at last filters through the Testarossa's cabin as we spot the sliproad we've been hunting for. Time to head towards Marrakesh.

I had been warned by regular visitors to Morocco that speed traps are rife on motorways and it's not long before we spot our first, only a few kilometres out of Tangier. We flash past a lonely policeman hiding in the undergrowth pointing a laser gun in our direction and, a kilometre or so later, it comes as no surprise when we're waved onto the hard shoulder by a group of armed and uniformed police officers for a 'chat'.

I knew we hadn't been speeding – I'd religiously stuck to the highway speed limit of 120km/h – but documents are demanded nonetheless. After a cursory glance, we are grudgingly waved on our way, only to find another speed trap just a little further down the road. Then another, and another. By the time we reach Marrakesh that evening, we reckon we have passed through 20 of them. A bit of a shock after 640 miles of freedom in Spain.

'We'd have no breakdown cover in Morocco, but the 4x4 drivers promised to help if we got into difficulty'

Above and right
Many of the road surfaces in Morocco are surprisingly smooth, but you have to expect to share them with everything from overloaded trucks to wandering camels.

'The policemen warn that the road ahead is in poor condition; one asks if I have a different car available'

The next morning, with the sun again beaming down on us out of a cloudless sky, photographer Justin Leighton arrives with *Octane*'s Matthew Hayward to join us on our adventure, having flown into Marrakesh overnight. Our plan is to head over the Atlas Mountains via the infamous Tiki Pass, after which we will turn slightly north-east to Ouarzazate and then on to Errachidia before turning south again, towards our destination of Erg Chebbi. The total distance for today's leg is estimated at 338 miles with a travel time of eight hours.

The hotel doorman had directed me to park in pride of place right outside the main entrance last night (apparently it's not often a Ferrari Testarossa visits Marrakesh) and, as it's a bit chilly this morning, I go to start the engine and warm its vital fluids before setting off. I twist the key, the starter spins, but the 12-cylinder eruption that should follow within a few seconds is absent. Oh dear, this wasn't in the script. Justin suggests it might be a good idea to order some tea.

It works because, while I down a delicious glass of Moroccan peppermint, I remember the car did this once before and it turned out that the left-hand distributor cap was a bit damp inside – and last night was the first time the Testarossa had spent a night al fresco in ages. I whip off the cap, give it a wipe, bolt it back into position, and the car starts straight away. The relief is palpable. Now we can begin our big adventure!

It's cost us an hour so we need to get a move on, and in the rush to get out of Marrakesh I forget to set up my digital speedo, which I instantly regret after getting pulled at the very first speed trap we come across for doing 69km/h in a 60 limit. The policemen can't quite believe I'm in a Ferrari and warn that the road ahead is in poor condition after the harsh winter, but at least it's open. One police officer takes me aside and asks if I have a different car available. I thank him for his helpful advice and, 300 dirham (£20) lighter, we press on towards the snow-capped Atlas Mountains in the distance. I've been itching for this section of road.

As it turns out, the climb towards the summit quickly becomes an anti-climax, as the route is choked by overloaded lorries grinding their way up almost at walking speed, so we stop at a fossil store and buy some crazy-coloured rocks to cheer ourselves up. The road surface as we near the top is terrible – a mix of mud, gravel and tarmac with hidden potholes – making overtaking next to impossible. This trip is going to be a whole lot tougher than I had expected.

But when we finally reach the 2260m (7415ft) summit, the sun breaks through the low cloud, the threatening snowflakes fade and the trucks dissipate as the road starts to twist its way down the other side of the mountain. Finally, I can begin to enjoy the Testarossa as Enzo intended, and soon the wail of 12 cylinders is bouncing off the rocky walls either side of the road. The further we drop, the better the road surface gets, and it's not long before the tedious trip out of Marrakesh becomes a distant memory.

With not a cloud in the sky, the scenery outside is ratcheting up from amazing to utterly stunning. Craggy cliffs that tower way above us mix with patches of cultivation in the valley below, and the glorious colours vary from a reddish-pink on the rocky mountain tops to a grey-green in the valleys far below.

Every now and then we come across gents wearing hooded cloaks (*djellabas*) gathering firewood or scrub and often riding donkeys. The further we blast along this road, the greater the contrast with the familiarity of Spain only a day or so earlier.

Some 125 miles after Marrakesh we stop for fuel (60p per litre!) in Ouarzazate, a town made famous as a film-making location. *Lawrence of Arabia* and *The Living Daylights* were shot here, and more recently the TV series *Game of Thrones*. And you can see why, as we sweep through the Vallée du Dades towards Errachidia. The overwhelming impression is of endless space, with nothing man-made or remotely modern to interfere with the extraordinary landscape rolling out in every direction.

We're starting to push on, yet the chances of reaching our planned overnight stop in the dunes of Errachidia are fading. Landmarks seem at least twice as far apart in reality as they did on the map, and our eight-hour estimate is proving hopelessly optimistic. At least the speed traps have finally disappeared and we meet the local constabulary only during random document checks into and out of towns along our route. I've also discovered a useful ploy: whenever we spot a police roadblock, tucking the Ferrari up behind Justin's Dacia hire car seems to lessen the chance of us being stopped.

The sun is sinking slowly into the horizon, signalling that we will soon be plunged into darkness – not good news, even though the Testarossa's quad-headlights are surprisingly good at piercing the inky night sky. No, the problem is that driving trucks, cars and bicycles without lights seems to be a national sport in Morocco, as is running across the road whenever foreign cars are approaching. By ten o'clock we've had enough of dodging endless errant cyclists and pedestrians in the middle of nowhere, so wearily we pull into Kasbah Chergui, the first hotel we spot as we drive into Erfoud, 40 miles short of our intended destination.

Fortunately we discover we've struck gold because the staff couldn't be more accommodating and open the kitchen to serve us a welcome supper, along with a glass or two of Domaine de Sahara Reserve red wine (which turns out to be surprisingly good). We retire happy, albeit with the prospect of an early start in the morning.

THE SAME CHEERFUL STAFF who served us supper treat us to a breakfast of traditional Moroccan pancakes with honey, followed by juicy chunks of melon, topped off with coffee thick enough to stand a spoon in. Fantastic. Outside, the sun is getting to work and the temperature is already heading towards today's promised 26-degree peak – not bad for mid-February. Refreshed, we pack our bags, clamber in and prepare to set off. But there's a problem. The Ferrari won't start again and cleaning the distributor cap doesn't do the trick this time, nor does the tea that Justin orders. This really is not good news, but there's no way I'm giving up now.

I whip out a spark plug and determine that no sparks are showing on either bank of cylinders, so I guess it's an immobiliser problem and start delving into the wiring to see if I can spot a fault somewhere. An hour or so later, with removed interior panels scattered around the place, we find a loose wire hidden behind the glovebox, and once it's re-connected the car fires up happily. Oh, the relief! We say our goodbyes to the hotel staff and get under way.

After 20 miles, an enormous arch marks the entrance to Rissani, the last outpost of civilisation before the tarmac road we're on runs out ten miles ahead of our final destination. Despite that, the road leading away from town is one of the best we've been on, arrow-straight for miles, its surface shimmering in the desert heat. It looks mighty tempting and, well, it would be rude not to: the Ferrari's throttle gets flattened, the engine note hardens and third gear is rapidly consumed.

Above and below
The ornate arch marks the entrance to Rissani, formerly a major (camel) caravan centre, and the last town before you reach the otherworldly landscape of the Sahara.

151

1987 Ferrari Testarossa

Engine 4943cc flat-12, DOHC per bank, Bosch K-Jetronic fuel injection
Power 390bhp @ 6300rpm
Torque 354bhp @ 4500rpm
Transmission Five-speed manual, rear-wheel drive **Steering** Rack and pinion **Suspension** Front and rear: double wishbones, coil springs, telescopic dampers, anti-roll bar
Brakes Discs **Weight** 1505kg
Top speed 178mph **0-60mph** 5.3sec

Above and right
These chaps are rather better suited to the environment than the Testarossa, but the car acquitted itself amazingly well, even on the brutally rough surfaces out towards the desert.

That oh-so-distinctive Ferrari flat-12 warble is demanding our full attention now, as is the way the horizon is rushing towards us. Click, clack, into fourth gear. Repeat. Yikes, this car can get a move on; it might feel slightly ponderous at lower speeds but it's higher up the speed range that the Testarossa really comes alive, almost untroubled by the volume of air it's having to push through.

As we round a bend, the pinkish-orange Sahara dunes finally loom on the horizon. The euphoria we feel at that moment is the same as you get when you've been at sea for days and then land suddenly appears. Just that brief glimpse of what lies ahead makes it seem worth travelling all this way. I sense this is going to be very special. The dunes look huge, even at this distance, and a few miles later we spot a rickety sign for the Hotel Yasmina pointing into the desert proper. The hotel is so remote it doesn't even have a street address, only a grid reference.

The owner of the Yasmina had promised me it would be possible to reach it with a two-wheel-drive car and, because it's where Richard Bremner and the F512 M stayed in 1995, I know at least one other Ferrari has made it there before.

Obstacles are few – the odd dried-up raven here, a rocky outcrop there – so four-wheel drive isn't really needed, but the track, while hard, is a vicious washboard surface. It shakes everything on the car to pieces, and my heart sinks at the realisation that there are ten miles of this to endure. Several Toyota Land Cruisers make a detour to check us out, their incredulous occupants smiling at what they're witnessing. I'm down to a crawl, shuffling along in second gear with the engine barely above tickover. It takes 40 minutes to complete this final leg of the journey, and even then we're not quite there because, from nowhere, a huge oasis appears in front of us, and there seems to be no way around it. Frustratingly, I can see the Yasmina in the distance.

By now, locals have got wind that there's a daft Englishman in a Ferrari lost in the Sahara and a couple of kids on beaten-up mopeds are zinging towards us. I climb out to explain in my best pidgin French that I'm trying to reach the Hotel Yasmina but don't know a good way to get there in the Testarossa. One offers to lead me there for a few dirham, to which I happily agree. It must be a bizarre sight: a single battered moped with its rider in traditional dress escorting a Ferrari over the uneven terrain. He takes us on a huge loop, riding up onto the stony banks surrounding the oasis and beckoning us to follow. I'm so glad the Testarossa wears relatively tall tyres because there's no way today's ultra-low-profiles would survive what we're doing right now.

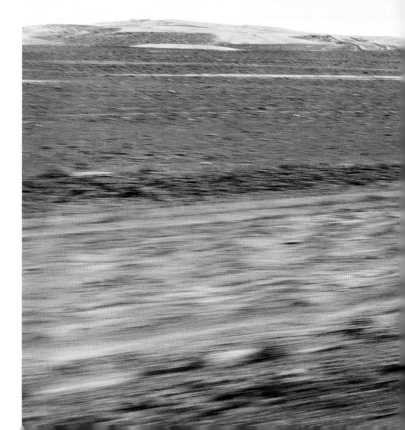

In fact, the Ferrari has proved to be a great companion on this trip, comfortable beyond expectation, unbelievably capacious for a mid-engined car, and only consuming a single litre of oil and absolutely no coolant throughout the whole trip. Even the air-conditioning has worked faultlessly – miraculous for an 1980s supercar in my experience. The roads in Morocco were way tougher than I had expected them to be, but the locals we met along the way were always extremely friendly and courteous, which helped lift our spirits. My guide on the moped ahead finally pulls over and cheerfully points towards the single-track bridge across to the hotel in front of us.

Wow. The scale, the beauty, the remoteness – it's almost too much. The Ferrari has made it, and I can't quite take it all in. We left our frosty gravel driveway at home in the Cotswolds only four days ago and now, some 2000 miles later, the stunning dunes of the Sahara are stretching out in front of me for thousands of miles and it looks utterly wonderful. There's the quiet satisfaction of finally achieving my personal goal of driving a Ferrari to the Sahara, just like Richard did. The difference, of course, is that he drove a brand-new car here with a degree of factory support hiding in the wings in case things went pear-shaped, while I drove a classic with just a minimal toolkit, a can of Radweld, a tow-rope and a credit card as back-up.

Given that we've got to turn around in a few days and drive all the way back home, there's plenty of time yet for my approach to be proven less than sensible, but there's no point in worrying about the return journey now. All I want to do is park up and enjoy our wonderful desert base to the full. After what we've been through to get here, I think we've earned it. ∎

OWNING A TESTAROSSA

Harry's Ferrari shares garage space with a Countach and 911 Turbo. So which is best?

I bought the Ferrari back in the summer of 2014 to sit alongside my 1987 Lamborghini Countach QV and 1989 Porsche 911 Turbo, completing my perfect '80s supercar trio.

The three cars couldn't be more different. The 911 is the everyday supercar, blending into the background when required but then delivering weapons-grade overtaking pace; the Countach is the stereotypical supercar best enjoyed in small doses; and the Testarossa sits somewhere in the middle, bridging both ends of the '80s supercar experience.

The Testarossa is the most modern of the three, too (both the Countach and Turbo date from the early '70s), the engine is untemperamental thanks to fuel injection (the V12 of the Countach is carb-fed), the air-con works, visibility out is fantastic, and the luggage space is vast thanks to the shelf behind the seats. We tested this by packing away a Moroccan bathroom sink, several large serving bowls and a set of fossil-encrusted dinner plates!

I chose a 1987 Testarossa because that year got the single-nut wheels (prettier than the later four-bolts) and the exhaust is pre-catalyst, so the engine sounds the best. Having now done this journey, I can see the Testarossa turning into my first choice for big trips, which is not something I would have predicted before I bought one. And that's why the Testarossa has turned out to be the most surprising supercar of the bunch.

2021 Ferrari F8 Spider
£249,950

1971 Ferrari 365 GTB-4 Daytona
£499,950

2003 Ferrari 575 Maranello F1 Fiorano Pack
£84,950

1985 Ferrari Testarossa 'Monospecchio'
£139,950

2015 Porsche 991 Turbo Coupe PDK
£88,950

2017 Ferrari California T
£119,950

2010 Lamborghini Gallardo LP570-4 Superleggera
£119,750

2017 McLaren 570 GT
£99,950

2021 Ferrari 812 GTS
£335,950

2017 Aston Martin DB11 V12
£94,950

1975 Kremer Porsche 911 Carrera 3.0 RSR
£695,000

2019 Aston Martin Vantage Coupe
£107,950

REDLINING

The F40 was the first production car to exceed 200mph.
In this mammoth group test, John Barker pits it against
its predecessor, and the even faster Ferraris that followed

Photography Matthew Howell

ANDY MORGAN

200

THE DOUBLE TON...

ALMOST 35 YEARS after Ferrari claimed the F40 to be the first production car able to crack 200mph, it's still a big number. For the record, the claim was 201mph. And, for the record, Guinness didn't recognise it.

This was not because the Italian magazine *Quattroruote* was the only publication to get an F40 to 200mph (several others tried and failed), but because its speed was eclipsed by RUF's 911-based CTR (211mph) and Porsche's 959 S (213mph). However, both of those stretch the notion of 'production' somewhat: only 29 of each were made while Ferrari went on to sell 1315 F40s.

Of all performance statistics, top speed is the least relevant. Yet it has always fascinated because it's such a simple concept. Every car enthusiast can remember the first time they hit 100mph (1982, A45 Ryton bypass, Jaguar XJ12, if you're asking), and the fastest they've ever driven (200mph, A9 autobahn, RUF Turbo R, 2003).

There's fame in being the fastest, too, which motivated the Italian manufacturers in particular during the 1960s. First came the Iso Grifo (161mph, disappointing given the claim of 185mph in my *Observer's Book of Automobiles*), before Lamborghini and Ferrari started slugging it out, trading the record back and forth over the next two decades: Miura P400 at 171mph, Daytona at 174mph, Countach LP400S and LP500S at 179mph and 182mph, and 288 GTO at 188mph.

The GTO is where we start this feature, because without it there would have been no F40. After that car, Ferrari left others to vie for the accolade of fastest production car. The F50 raised the Ferrari bar just a fraction to 202mph, while the Enzo claimed an enigmatic '217mph-plus'. Just over a decade later, the 950bhp LaFerrari claimed the same. And why not? As made clear by an extraordinary day in the company of Ferrari's greatest supercars, 200 is plenty.

2013 Ferrari 458 Challenge race car.

Great track car with proven race winning history, fitted with the Bamd aero kit, including rear carbon spoiler + diffusers. New steel disc brakes with the original carbon brakes retained. Silencers fitted to exhausts; originals retained. Upgraded anti-roll bar, 2-way adjustable dampers. 3 sets of wheels, full PPF coating, spare windscreen and removable passenger seat. Only 4,705km. **£120,000**.

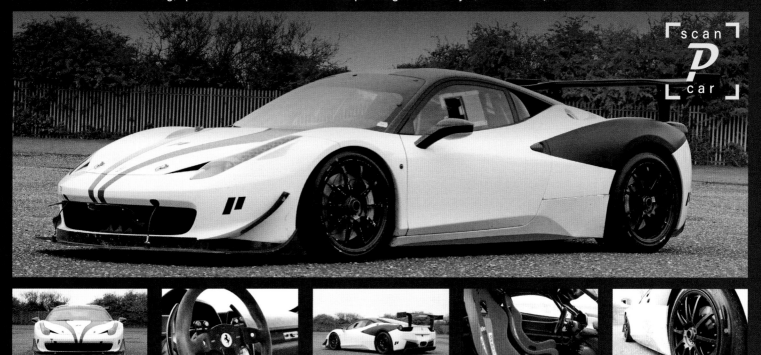

[scan P car]

1972 Ferrari Daytona 365 GTB/4.

All matching numbers and owned by the same family since 1976. One of only 158 UK RHD cars produced, 1284 in total. Well-documented history, fully maintained with original owner's manual, bodywork spare parts catalogues and original tool bag. Finished in the Rosso Corsa with Pelle beige and red leather. 38,000 genuine miles. **£515,000**.

HALL & HALL

Graham Hill Way, Bourne, Lincolnshire. PE10 9PJ

01778 392562
vince@hallandhall.net
www.hallandhall.net

P
PRESTIGE DRIVER™
Available on the App Store   GET IT ON Google Play

THIS TRIO, NOSE TO TAIL, is like an automotive version of the ascent of man, the evolution from ape to *homo sapiens*. There's a visual gulf between the bookends, the curvy 288 GTO having the ground clearance of an off-roader compared with the sharp-edged, road-hugging F40. It looks like they're separated by a decade when in fact it's just a couple of years. And sitting between them is the missing link, the 288 GTO Evoluzione.

I still can't get over how the demands of competition produced a car as beautiful as the GTO, and it's as good to drive as it is to look at. It's as accomplished an everyday road car as the Porsche 959 that was expected to be its competition rival. Both were designed to meet the Group B regulations introduced by motorsport's governing body, FISA, in 1982.

It was probably Ferrari's and Porsche's reluctance to compromise on general habitability, driveability and build quality that contributed to their both missing the Group B boat. For homologation, 200 cars had to be built for sale to the public, and the rally fraternity got there much more quickly. The first fully formed, mid-engined, four-wheel-drive Group B special, Peugeot's 205 T16, was ready for the opening stages of the 1985 World Rally Championship. A year later, several terrible accidents saw Group B abandoned.

Ferrari showed the 288 GTO at Geneva in early 1984 and launched the Testarossa at Paris in October. Two more different big-horsepower Ferraris you cannot conceive: the flat-12 Testarossa was an evolution of the 512 BB, the GTO came from the racing department. Harvey Postlethwaite took the 308 GTB, turned its V8 through 90 degrees and gave it a pair of turbos. The end-on gearbox lengthened the wheelbase, and wider tracks demanded a restyle.

In 1977, Pininfarina had proposed some aerodynamic improvements for the 308 with its Millechiodi concept. *Millechiodi* translates as 'one thousand nails' – a reference to the many rivets that secured the various addenda. Some of them were adopted in mild form by the 308 QV, but the GTO went the whole way with the shovel-like front spoiler, the kicked-up tail and the distended arches.

Chief engineer Nicola Materazzi was in charge of the turbocharging. He lobbied for Japanese IHI turbos rather than the products of Ferrari's incumbent supplier, KKK, successfully demonstrating that the IHI units were better matched to the engine. The flat-plane-crank V8 had a slightly reduced bore, dropping its capacity from 2927cc to 2855cc. When multiplied by FISA's turbocharged equivalency factor of 1.4, the engine capacity came in just below the specified 4000cc limit. Strictly speaking the engine was a 2.9, but '298 GTO' just didn't have the same ring to it.

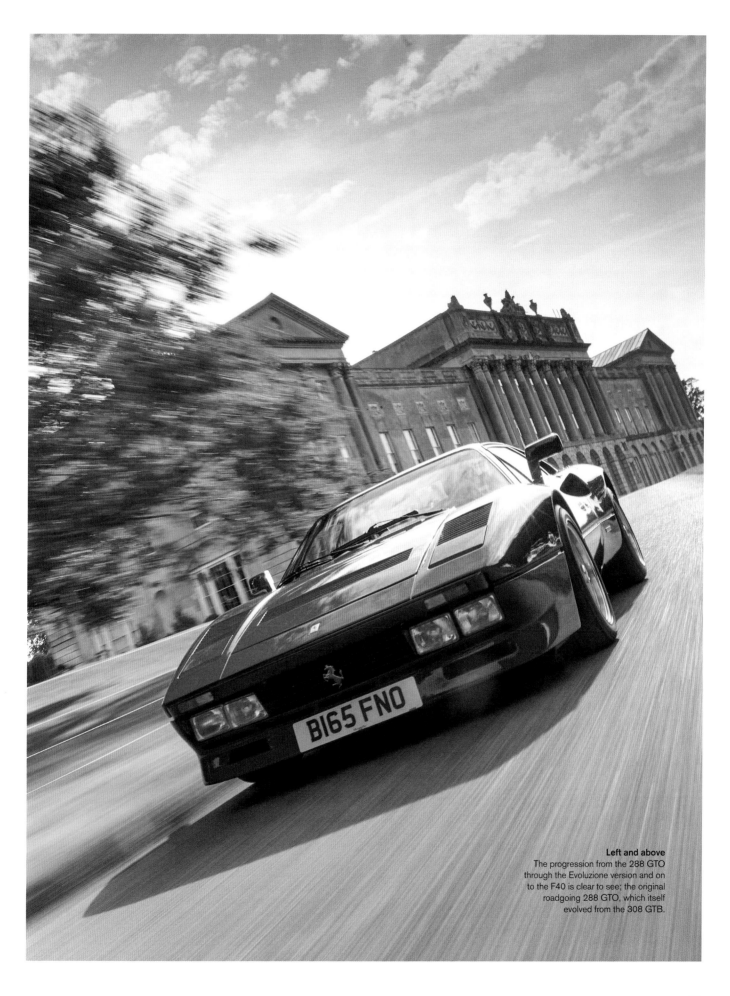

Left and above
The progression from the 288 GTO
through the Evoluzione version and on
to the F40 is clear to see; the original
roadgoing 288 GTO, which itself
evolved from the 308 GTB.

FOR YEARS, THE GTO has been my dream car, my lottery-win car. It would need to be a solid EuroMillions win today, but when I first drove a GTO 16 years ago it still cost less than my house. I was terrified that I would be disappointed after so many years of fantasising, but I needn't have worried. It exceeded all my expectations.

So it's wonderful to get behind the wheel again but, first, let's deal with what's wrong. You sit a bit high. Too bad. And now, the rest…

In the mid-'80s, the world hadn't yet become obsessed with low-profile tyres and the stiff suspension needed to exploit them, so the GTO has a well-controlled, supple ride that allows it to roll into corners. But what really gives a sense of what the car is doing is the non-assisted steering. The GTO is proof that, even with fat 225/55 ZR16 front tyres, you can have completely manageable, accurate and wonderfully tactile steering without power assistance. The GTO has such an effortless gait, parrying bumps and hollows, that you can unleash more of its performance more of the time.

Given the outputs Materazzi coaxed from this engine for the Evoluzione, the GTO's 394bhp sounds quite tame. It doesn't feel it. Up to about 3000rpm there's the sound of a gathering storm, the low rumble of the engine gradually joined by the sound of ever-increasing amounts of air being ingested. Then the turbos kick in, the GTO squats a little and

you're off, riding a wave of boost right up to 7000rpm. With the rear tyres secure on warm, dry asphalt, the power is addictively exploitable. We had an Enzo along when I first drove the GTO, and on a bumpy, fast Welsh B-road the Enzo had to drop back because its underside kept hitting the road. For me, that cemented the 288's hero status. It's so good that it's hard to believe this was simply the car Ferrari had to make so it could homologate the Evoluzione, our next car here.

When Group B got canned, work on the Evoluzione halted. At that point there were three examples – two built from scratch and one converted from a 288 GTO. Sub-contractor Michelotto later built three more for favoured clients, and our example here is the first of those.

It seems incredible, but Ferrari had plans to rally the GTO. Materazzi was developing a 550bhp engine that gave maximum torque at 3800rpm for rallying, and a peakier 650bhp version for racing. The minimum weight for cars in Group B's 4000cc class was 1100kg, which would have allowed Ferrari to place a lot of ballast strategically because the Evoluzione had a dry weight of just 960kg. That's a massive 200kg less than the regular GTO, itself quite a lightweight thanks to the use of composite materials.

You can see where some of the savings are. Windscreen apart, the windows are all plastic, with holes. You can feel it, too: you have so little mass to work against when you swing the door open that you feel as clumsy as the Incredible Hulk.

Clockwise from far left
The Evoluzione version of the 288 shows its wider track and exposed engine; the regular GTO is almost luxurious in comparison; drilled plastic windows, side gussets and 650bhp on tap in the Evo.

1984 Ferrari 288 GTO

Engine 2855cc mid-mounted V8, flat-plane crankshaft, DOHC per bank, 32 valves, two IHI turbochargers, Weber-Marelli IAW engine management **Power** 394bhp @ 7000rpm **Torque** 366lb ft @ 3800rpm **Transmission** Five-speed manual transaxle, rear-wheel drive **Steering** Rack and pinion **Suspension** Front and rear: double wishbones, coil springs, anti-roll bar **Brakes** Ventilated discs **Weight** 1160kg **Top speed** 188mph **0-62mph** 4.8sec

1986 Ferrari 288 GTO Evoluzione

Engine 2855cc mid-mounted V8, flat-plane crankshaft, DOHC per bank, 32 valves, two IHI turbochargers, Weber-Marelli IAW engine management **Power** 650bhp @ 7800rpm **Torque** N/A **Transmission** Five-speed manual transaxle, rear-wheel drive **Steering** Rack and pinion **Suspension** Front and rear: double wishbones, coil springs, anti-roll bar **Brakes** Ventilated discs **Weight** 940kg **Top speed** 225mph **0-62mph** N/A

All the composite bodywork is thinned down, the rear clamshell is peppered with vents to let the heat out, and the other panels wear scoops and NACA ducts to get the air in. And then it strikes you that all of the vents and ducts on the Evoluzione are in exactly the same place on the F40 sitting alongside. Even the height of the rear spoiler and the slightly shovel-snout front are copied across. No question, the Evoluzione has more in common with the F40 than the 288 GTO that spawned it.

Wedged and belted into the snug, deep-sided bucket seat, I see more similarities such as the felt-covered facia and the carbonfibre box-sections leading into the footwells. The mismatched collection of dials ahead shows the important stuff – revs, boost and oil pressure – while hanging off the bottom edge of the facia in its own binnacle is the speedo. I'm as apprehensive as I am excited about the prospect of 650 turbocharged horsepower in less than 1000kg of Ferrari.

The noise that erupts from behind when the squidgy black start button is pressed doesn't help. A thrummy, rumbling, gnashing cacophony fills the bare cockpit, but that's nothing. Get going, and the maniacal whine of straight-cut gears slices though you like some experimental Cold War weapon designed to liquidise your soft tissues.

There won't be a chance to open up the Evoluzione fully as we're restricted to the roads of the estate where we're photographing the cars. But there are tantalising glimpses of its potential, moments when the revs rise and the boost starts to build with an urgent hissing before an explosion of torque fires the Evoluzione up the road like a steam catapult. The overrun noise is a grin-making chatter of chuffs as excess boost is blown off.

Driving this car some years ago, accomplished racer Tony Dron reckoned the challenge was to exploit all of the immense performance available. 'It's the sudden rush of power that demands you take the Evo seriously,' he said. 'Put your foot down hard a moment too early, and all hell could be let loose.'

I might not have felt its full force on this occasion, but by the end of the day I'll have tried something rather similar.

Right
These three manifestations of a particular Ferrari gene pool are more similar than their creators might have liked us to think.

'THE F40 IS MORE FEROCIOUS THAN THE GTO. IT TAKES ALL YOUR COURAGE TO KEEP IT NAILED'

GIVEN THE F40's iconic status today, it's hard to believe that when it was launched in 1987 many commentators considered it a rather cynical car, built to cash in on the first financial boom and the demand for Porsche's £150,000 959. Ferrari dismissed these accusations, saying that the F40 was for customers who wanted nothing but sheer performance. 'It isn't a laboratory for the future,' said Ferrari's marketing man, 'and it wasn't created because Porsche made the 959. It would have happened anyway.'

That last assertion may well be true. After all, a chunk of the development was already done. With the Evoluzione, Ferrari's engineering brains had worked out how to get much more power from the twin-turbo V8, how to configure the cooling requirements and the aerodynamics. That's how they were able to bring the F40 to market in just 13 months.

The F40 was essentially a stripped-out, hotted-up 288 GTO, built on the same tubular steel chassis with some Kevlar/carbon panels bonded to it. Gordon Murray, then planning the McLaren F1, was famously disparaging, pointing out that its chassis was very old-tech. And, yes, it was expensive: in the UK it cost £193,000, more than twice what the GTO had cost.

Designer Leonardo Fioravanti had been given many hard points to work to, including where all the scoops and ducts and vents were to go, but the shape that he created was shocking and exciting, from its low nose to its high-rise wing. Then there were the stats: 478bhp, making it just a bit more powerful than the 959, and a top speed of 201mph, making it just a bit faster and also (drum roll) the first production car with a claimed top speed of over 200mph.

There's always a sense of occasion as you fall as gracefully as you can into the embrace of the deep-sided, red-fabric seat. You sit lower than in the GTO, so the steering wheel feels higher and more canted away from you, more kart-like. The cabin is bare like a race car's: hollow doors with pull strings, drilled pedals and exposed Kevlar/carbon in the footwells that looks like it's bonded at the joins with daubs of green bathroom sealer.

However, the car isn't as stiff or edgy or spiky as you expect; it's is a bit like meeting a skinhead and finding he's rather well-mannered. I've had colleagues who finally get behind the wheel and are actually disappointed that it's not wilder. But given how many F40s have been crashed and how many change hands quickly, their owners having frightened themselves, it's probably plenty scary enough.

Thumb the starter button, which is like the fuel primer on a petrol mower, and the cockpit fills with the busy, impatient *blat-blat-blat* of the flat-plane V8. As you give the heavy throttle an exploratory squeeze, the note swells and get thrashier. There's a satisfying matching of control weights and feel; the unassisted steering, brake and gearshift are all similarly hefty and tactile.

Forget second gear from cold. When it's ready to play, the engine will be about ready to go, too, so find a safe space and get the throttle to the floor. The F40 doesn't disappoint. It's more ferocious, louder and hissier than the GTO, and it takes all your courage to keep it nailed – especially if there are bumps, because it's stiffer, too, though still not tough. And if the rear tyres got loose…

I'm always amazed at how driveable an 1100kg car with a 470bhp turbocharged V8 and no traction control really is. You have to build up to it, work out where the boost comes in and how fiercely, but if you're comfortable with opposite lock and have a sense of when the rear tyres are going to struggle with the spike in torque, you can ride it out and it's very satisfying. Factory test driver Dario Benuzzi and his team did a great job of slowing things down at the limit, so that things don't have to escalate beyond your control.

Pick your corner, give it a fixed amount of throttle, wait for the boost to arrive, wind on the lock to catch it as it does, hold your nerve and some yards up the road the boost will tail off and the status quo will be restored. There will also be two black lines on the road, but you won't be able to see them through the vented rear screen.

The 288 GTO was designed for competition but was never raced. The F40, ironically, was designed purely for the road but soon found itself on starting grids around the world. The factory protested at first but relented under pressure from Daniel Marin, manager of France's Ferrari importer, and engineer Materazzi, who wanted to exploit all the car's potential. The factory's go-to specialist, Michelotto, obliged, producing what was known initially as the F40 LM and later as the Competizione, because the factory thought the LM moniker limited its appeal.

It featured a comprehensive package of upgrades, including lightweight bodywork and a heavy-hitting, 700bhp-plus engine that could, apparently, produce up to 900bhp for qualifying. But before we light that particular firework, let's warm up with a stepping-stone: the F40 GT.

Left and above
Three versions of the
F40. The LM (in the
foreground) was raced
in the 1990 IMSA
championship; the GT
is a Group N car and
is almost standard.

WITH ITS BRIGHT white alloys and smattering of decals, the F40 GT looks a much more serious car than the standard F40. But it's in effect a Group N racer, so very lightly modified – a skinhead with tattoos, if you like. This car competed in the Italian GT championship for three seasons from 1992 in the hands of Pierre Popoff, a good friend of Enzo, winning a couple of rounds in '94. It was then converted for road use. In 2013 it was restored to its original race spec, which involved refitting a race exhaust and Brembo race brakes, converting the car to run on its original magnesium alloys and, of course, recreating its livery.

It retained its road-car suspension bushing because it was going to continue being used on the road. And I have to say it drives beautifully, better than the stock road car. Is this the result of three seasons of development that kept it racing competitively? Maybe. The brake and throttle are closer together, aiding heel-and-toe shifts, and the gearshift is free of the friction that makes some F40 shifts harder work.

I wonder if the larger-diameter, suede-trimmed Momo is there for leverage, to make slicks more manageable. Whatever, the upshot is steering that's lighter and a car that's more biddable. Add an engine that comes on boost more progressively – which would help when exiting the Parabolica on the limit of grip with a 911 or an XJ220 up your chuff – and you have a very sweet F40. The best I've driven, in fact.

Then there's the F40 LM. Until I got up close, I hadn't appreciated quite how serious a race car it was, or its history. I'd clocked the fixed headlamps, the adjustable rear wing

and the aggressive stance. I'd even noted the Lime Rock scrutineering ticket, but until I dropped my backside into this car I hadn't recognised the most out-of-place detail: the number plate.

A number plate. I can laugh now. The Lime Rock sticker was the last the car wore in the 1990 IMSA championship, which saw it raced by a few folk you might have heard of – Hurley Haywood, Jacques Laffite, Jean-Louis Schlesser, Michel Ferté… This is the second of the 19 cars built, so a genuine LM, and it scored podium finishes at Mid Ohio and Mosport. It's got a reputed 760bhp and now I'm going to drive it on some British A- and B-roads.

Ahead of the removable Momo is a race-spec Magneti Marelli digital display. To the right, the felt dash is studded with an array of buttons and knobs, most of which I hope I won't need (extinguishers, brake bias adjusters and suchlike). I flick the starter switch, the starter motor whines double-time, and in an instant the engine is fast-idling busily behind me. I can't decipher much of the digital dash so I decide to take the LM on the same run as the other cars, so I'll have an idea of what it's like once warmed up. That's if I can stop stalling it; the clutch is like a light switch. The car also has the turning circle of a supertanker and, like all F40s, woeful rear visibility. I'm sweating before I've escaped the courtyard.

After 15 minutes I accept that there is no smooth way of changing gear with the straight-cut 'box, only degrees of violence as the teeth mesh as smoothly as a rugby scrum.

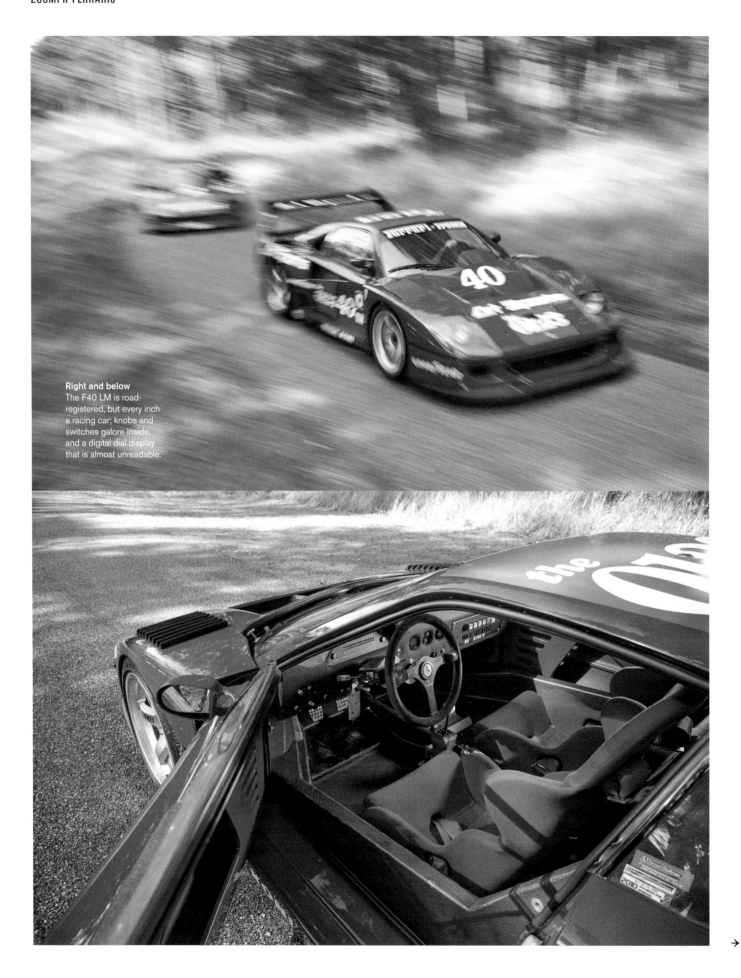

Right and below
The F40 LM is road-registered, but every inch a racing car; knobs and switches galore inside, and a digital dial display that is almost unreadable.

1987 Ferrari F40

Engine 2936cc mid-mounted V8, flat-plane crankshaft, DOHC per bank, 32 valves, two IHI turbochargers, Weber-Marelli IAW engine management **Power** 478bhp @ 7000rpm **Torque** 426lb ft @ 4000rpm **Transmission** Five-speed manual transaxle, rear-wheel drive **Steering** Rack and pinion **Suspension** Front and rear: double wishbones, coil springs, anti-roll bar **Brakes** Ventilated discs **Weight** 1100kg **Top speed** 201mph **0-62mph** 4.1sec

1992 Ferrari F40 GT

Engine 2936cc mid-mounted V8, flat-plane crankshaft, DOHC per bank, 32 valves, two IHI turbochargers, Weber-Marelli IAW engine management **Power** 478bhp @ 7000rpm **Torque** 426lb ft @ 4000rpm **Transmission** Five-speed manual transaxle, rear-wheel drive **Steering** Rack and pinion **Suspension** Front and rear: double wishbones, coil springs, anti-roll bar **Brakes** Ventilated discs **Weight** 1100kg **Top speed** 201mph **0-62mph** 4.1sec

1987 Ferrari F40 LM

Engine 2936cc mid-mounted V8, flat-plane crankshaft, DOHC per bank, 32 valves, two IHI turbochargers, Weber-Marelli IAW engine management **Power** 760bhp @ 8100rpm **Torque** N/A **Transmission** Five-speed manual transaxle, rear-wheel drive **Steering** Rack and pinion **Suspension** Front and rear: double wishbones, coil springs, anti-roll bar **Brakes** Ventilated discs **Weight** 1050kg **Top speed** 228mph **0-62mph** N/A

I'm worried that I won't get to feel the full performance because the V8 falters a bit between 3000 and 4000rpm, but when I find an empty straight and sink the throttle in second gear, the V8 clears its throat after 4000rpm and starts to build boost at about 5000rpm. Big boost, fast.

The sound of air being sucked in is now fighting for dominance with the V8's light beat. The sound and the shove suddenly escalate and at about 6000rpm (who knows; I'm not looking) there's a devastating explosion of torque. We jump into hyperspace, the scenery now reversing past the Lexan side windows in a soupy green blur as the air is squeezed from my chest. Then my right foot lifts and we are wrapped in normality again.

Oh. My. God. I've driven lots of very fast cars and this is as BANG!-fast, fill-your-pants-scary as any of them.

I go in search of big, smooth, wide roads. Third gear to minimise the risk of wheelspin, the pedal goes to the floor and stays there. We take off at 6000rpm, the acceleration shifting us into another tunnel-like reality, and a moment later I register that the V8 is banging its head against the 8000rpm limiter. I grab fourth just to calm things, the straight-cut gears engage with the sound of a door slamming and I release the throttle. I check the door mirrors expecting to see the tarmac behind rucked up like a Wall's Viennetta.

I know it would wear slicks on track, and as well as a 900bhp qualifying tune there was probably a softer tune for wet running, but seriously, what an absolute weapon the F40 LM is. And what a privilege to have spent an hour in it, finding smooth, meandering roads and massive junctions to turn around in, and still not getting anywhere near comfortable with the explosive delivery, the astonishing brutality. This is the full-on, cage-fighter F40. It shouldn't really be on the road, but it's fantastic that it is.

'THE F50'S STOCK WAS HIGHER WITH OWNERS THAN WITH THE PRESS, WHO DROVE IT JUST A FEW LAPS AT FIORANO'

Above
The F50 (right) has
a carbonfibre shell
like the LaFerrari (left),
but predates the hybrid
hypercar by nearly
two decades; the Enzo
(centre) sacrifices much
in the way of practicality
for savage performance.

HOW DO YOU FOLLOW the F40? With a car that's much more technically advanced and delivers, said Ferrari, 'the emotion of Formula 1' thanks in part to an F1-derived V12. Yet the F50 also claims the title of Maranello's most misunderstood supercar. In fairness, the F50's stock was a lot higher with owners than with the press, not least because initially the factory allowed journalists to drive just a handful of laps at Fiorano. And then there was how it looked. Not since the XJ-S replaced the E-type had there been a more disappointing follow-up.

It was a four-wheeled contradiction. Its skeleton was an aerospace-built carbon tub, and its heart was derived from the 3.5-litre engine used in the 1989 F1 season, the first of the post-turbo era. The V12 had ditched the pneumatic valves and 14,000rpm redline and had grown to 4.7 litres, but it was bolted directly to the tub and together with its six-speed transaxle was a load-bearing structure, supporting the inboard suspension, rear bumper and bodywork. Hardcore, then. But its body styling was softcore, lacking the aggression of the F40, so much smoother, swoopier and… convertible.

It didn't stack up for me. Then, in 2004, I drove one and

it did. Up against the 288 GTO, the F40 and the Enzo in that *evo* magazine group test, the F50 came out on top. By consensus. It didn't displace the 288 GTO as my favourite Ferrari supercar, but I appreciated why it had won. Compared with the turbocharged cars it was raw and direct, with a compelling, steely-edged mechanical and dynamic fidelity that engaged and rewarded. Oh, and its V12 revved thrillingly to 8500rpm and its gearshift and non-assisted steering were sublime.

Fifteen years on, 520bhp is no big deal, but what remains striking is the lack of, well, everything. The interior is largely uninterrupted swathes of glossy carbonfibre and grey Alcantara, with dimpled rubber flooring. There's no radio, the windows are wind-up, and the slim centre console houses just a couple of air-con dials, a handbrake and the open gate of a carbon-topped gearlever. Everything you need and no more.

The V12 idles smoothly with a complex beat and your seat shakes like it's bolted to it, which in effect it is. A dab of throttle sees the revs flare and die in an instant, like a motorbike engine, while the seat fizzes. Despite a linkage

over six feet long with four UJs, the gearshift is more tactile and slicker than in any of the V8 cars. You end up rev-matching every shift not because you need to, but because it's a pleasure.

The engine is a gem, too. It lacks the low-end torque of the V8s so you have to work to find the power but, boy, is it rewarding work. The free-revving V12 has a thrilling, manic top-end that you can fully exploit because the chassis is so much more supple and composed than the F40's. The heft of the manual steering never quite leaves it, but it's manageable and full of feel, as are the unassisted brakes.

The F50 is an absolute joy going fast or slow, a beautifully polished, tactile and exploitable machine. It's not as brutally fast or as exquisitely made as the other all-carbon, race-inspired V12 supercar that grabbed so much attention in the 1990s, but – shock – the F50 is way better to drive than the McLaren F1.

ON PAPER THE Enzo looks like an evolution of the F50. Parked next to it, the Enzo looks like an alien spacecraft. It's such a three-dimensional design, its plump, diamond-shaped centre slung between pontoons housing the wheels. Pull up a dihedral door and the cockpit looks alien, too, a complex, gappy amalgam of parts, like a Lego kit trying to do curvy, peppered with buttons and dials and switches. There's no gearlever here, shifting duties being assigned to carbonfibre paddles and an automated, single-plate clutch, but we have power assistance for steering and brakes,

Clockwise from left
The F50 (nose in the foreground) wasn't quite the looker many had hoped for, and the strange beauty of the Enzo (background) was polarising; the LaFerrari (foreground) is a surprisingly easy car to drive; the Enzo is older than you think: 400 were built from 2002 to 2004.

'IN THE ENZO, TRACTION CONTROL IS AN ESSENTIAL, NOT MERELY A NICE-TO-HAVE'

ASR (traction control) and a collection of coloured mode buttons on the steering wheel that in future Ferraris will coalesce into the now-ubiquitous *manettino* toggle switch.

The Enzo also introduced the new six-litre F140 V12, and what an astonishing engine it is. Smoother, more bassy and more musical than the F50's V12, it also feels twice as potent, as I rediscover with a start the first time I squeeze the throttle and the back end shimmies. It delivers 660bhp, plus 485lb ft of torque at 5500rpm, but I reckon most of that torque is available from just over tickover. ASR is an essential, not merely a nice-to-have; goad the F40 and eventually it'll bite, but the Enzo's V12 has so much grunt that its fat Bridgestones don't stand a chance.

There's more to come from the V12 but first you have to adapt to the steering, which is assisted and manageable but rather lacking in feel; and to the gearshift, which offers brilliant rev-matched downshifts but feels long-winded on upshifts. Or brutal if you don't bother to lift. After the F50, it feels like you've traded in a lot for stupendous performance.

But stupendous it is. Tickover to 8000rpm is an emotional journey, the character and tone of the V12 softening then swelling then softening again before the revs rise ever more confidently until they reach 6000rpm and it feels like an afterburner has kicked in. The F50's V12 is manic enough over the last couple of thousand revs, but the Enzo destroys it, rearranging your underwear. Just keep an eye out for bumps because, excellent as the ride is, that long nose is vulnerable to scuffing.

I'D LOVE TO HAVE been in the meeting at Maranello where it was decided that what the successor to the Enzo needed was another 300bhp. I guess there were some outside factors influencing the decision, namely the McLaren P1 and the Porsche 918, cars with 916 and 893bhp respectively. And so, in 2013, a little over a decade after the F50 was launched, Ferrari announced the 963bhp LaFerrari.

The good news is that at its heart was an evolution of the Enzo's V12, now enlarged to 6.3 litres and developing a mighty 800bhp. Add in 120kw (163bhp) of electric power

Left, from top
The Enzo's thrilling 660bhp V12. In the LaFerrari, an engine based on the Enzo's is paired with a KERS system to make a staggering 963bhp; the dashboard of the newer car is ultra-simple at rest.

from the KERS (Kinetic Energy Recovery System) and you get a sensational 963bhp at 9000rpm. The LaFerrari weighs 1480kg in its lightest form – that's a little over 100kg heavier than the Enzo, but impressive given the weight of the KERS, its attendant batteries and the bulkier double-clutch gearbox.

With the key in your hand, you're buzzing as you walk towards the LaFerrari, high on an emotional cocktail that's two parts anxiety, two parts excitement. The car is worth around £2m and it's got an even higher power-to-weight ratio than the ballistic F40 LM. At least it has stability control and anti-lock brakes, I tell myself. Release the dihedral door and there's almost a foot of asphalt to step across to get to the slim, carbonfibre tub. Drop into the Alcantara-trimmed bucket seat, tug on the parachute handle to pull yourself closer to the pedals, and unexpectedly the pedals glide smoothly towards you.

Dead ahead is an evolution of the Enzo wheel with the manettino and... a quartic rim. I wasn't expecting that. It helps frame the digital instrument pack and suggests a super-fast steering ratio requiring no more than a handful of lock. The V12 fires, its bass voice competing with a collection of whines and hums for vocal dominance. Deep breath.

Here's the thing. The LaFerrari is easy to drive. It's a comfortable car with good forward visibility (in the rear view mirror, you can see the engine better than the road). Its steering has good weighting and is measured in its response, not too sharp away from centre. Its gearbox is as

1995 Ferrari F50

Engine 4699cc mid-mounted V12, DOHC per bank, 60 valves, Bosch Motronic engine management **Power** 520bhp @ 8500rpm **Torque** 347lb ft @ 6500rpm **Transmission** Six-speed manual transaxle, rear-wheel drive **Steering** Rack and pinion **Suspension** Front and rear: double wishbones, inboard coil spring/damper units with pushrods and rocker arms, anti-roll bar, variable electronic dampers **Brakes** Ventilated discs **Weight** 1230kg **Top speed** 202mph **0-62mph** 3.7sec

2002 Enzo Ferrari

Engine 5998cc mid-mounted V12, DOHC per bank, 48 valves, Bosch Motronic engine management **Power** 660bhp @ 7800rpm **Torque** 485lb ft @ 5500rpm **Transmission** Six-speed sequential semi-auto transaxle, rear-wheel drive **Steering** Rack and pinion, power-assisted **Suspension** Front and rear: double wishbones, inboard coil spring/damper units with pushrods and rocker arms, anti-roll bar, variable electronic dampers **Brakes** Ventilated carbon-ceramic discs **Weight** 1365kg **Top speed** 217mph **0-62mph** 3.7sec

2013 LaFerrari

Engine 6262cc mid-mounted V12, DOHC per bank, 48 valves, Bosch Motronic management, plus electric motor **Power** V12: 800bhp @ 9000rpm; electric motor 163bhp **Torque** V12: 516lb ft @ 6750rpm **Transmission** Seven-speed sequential semi-auto double-clutch transaxle, rear-wheel drive **Steering** Rack and pinion, power-assisted **Suspension** Inboard coil spring/damper units with pushrods and rocker arms, anti-roll bar, variable electronic dampers. Double wishbones at front, multi-link system at rear **Brakes** Ventilated carbon-ceramic discs **Weight** 1480kg **Top speed** 217mph **0-62mph** 3.0sec

'IT'S RELENTLESS, THE AMAZING GEARBOX CHANGING UP AT 9000RPM WITH NO BREAK IN THE ONSLAUGHT'

discreet and accommodating as a butler, and lumps and bumps disappear beneath the wheels noiselessly. Only the brake feel spoils the party, being a little inconsistent underfoot, presumably as electric regeneration and regular hydraulics divvy up the stopping duties. And then a half-hearted prod of the throttle summons up instantaneous and enormous urge. It's a shock; I was expecting some kind of build-up.

That's the contribution of the KERS: Ferrari has used the instantaneous response of the electric motor to sharpen throttle response and bolster the V12's low-end torque. It works brilliantly, the delivery surreally crisp. And while you occasionally sense the faint, steadying hand of traction control, there's obviously good mechanical grip as well.

Keep it pinned and the big V12 soon gets into its stride, its shove ramping up and up until it's into dizzying, *Looney Tunes* territory. It's relentless, the amazing gearbox changing up at 9000rpm with no break in the accelerative onslaught, and the desire to see how long that push is sustained is hard to resist. The LaFerrari is a staggering piece of engineering, and it raises just one question: what on Earth comes next?

BEING ASKED which of these eight Ferraris is best is like being asked to choose your favourite child, but I'll give it a go. I still love the rarity, looks and everyday usability of the 288 GTO, and the surprising exploitability and sense of occasion of the F40. The F40 LM racer is one of the most explosively powerful cars I've ever driven on the road, and you've got to love the absurdity of it.

The Enzo gets wilder with the passing years; it's a complex sculpture of a car and its potent V12 is so rich in character that you never tire of using it. The LaFerrari elevates the Ferrari supercar to a whole new level. But, against all my expectations, I have a new favourite: the F50. I still can't love the looks, but in every other way it has it all – a thrilling, vocal, easily exploited V12, a sublime manual shift, superb steering and dynamics that encourage you to press on to 200mph given the chance. Or just enjoy it at an amble. **End**

THANKS TO Will Kitchener and everyone at Heveningham Hall for the spectacular location. The 2022 Heveningham Concours is on 2-3 July (heveninghamconcours.com). Thanks also to Tom Cribb of Cascais Classics (cascaisclassics.com).

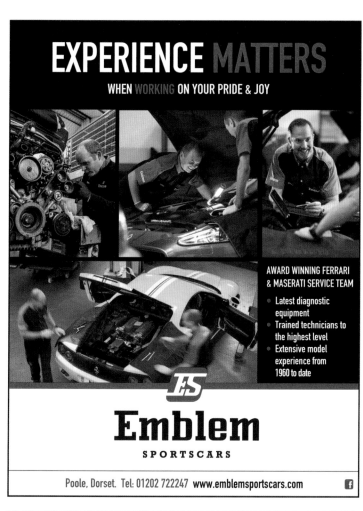
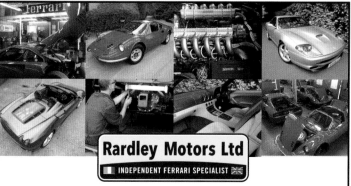

1996 SPANISH GRAND PRIX

THE REIGN IN SPAIN

In atrocious conditions at the 1996 Spanish GP,
Michael Schumacher produced an unforgettable drive

Words Andrew Frankel   **Photography** LAT

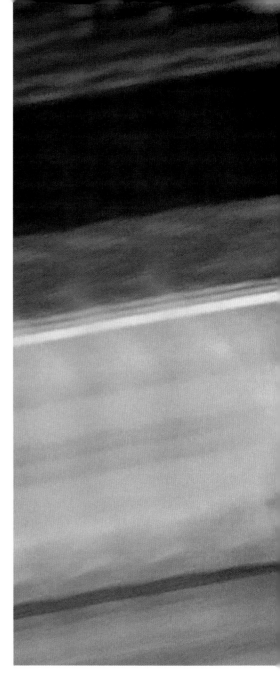

Sometimes the meaning of words changes according to who is saying them. Take this quote about Michael Schumacher's performance in the 1996 Spanish Grand Prix: 'That was not a race. That was a demonstration of brilliance. The man is in a class of his own. There is no-one in the world anywhere near him. I do not think there has ever been a driver who is so far clear of the field in terms of ability. It was one of the most fantastic demonstrations of skill I have ever seen, up there with Senna and Fangio.'

Had they been uttered by, say, Schumacher's manager, Willi Weber, we might not take them seriously. Spoken by Stirling Moss, inarguably one of the greatest racing drivers of all time, they mean something else altogether – and looking back at what Schumacher did in Barcelona that day, it is impossible to accuse Sir Stirling of hyperbole.

BUT FIRST a little context. By the time that Schumacher joined the Scuderia for the start of the 1996 season, he was already a double World Champion, the man who had vanquished the seemingly insuperable Williams team with Benetton. By way of contrast, Ferrari was in the middle of its longest drought since the start of the Formula 1 World Championship in 1950. Not since the 1979 season had one of its drivers carried off F1's ultimate prize.

A Drivers' Championship is a child of many parents, and it would take Ferrari until the turn of the century to assemble a team to properly complement Schumacher's gifts. It was not realistic to think the German could challenge for the title in 1996. But a single race? A single race Schumacher could win, by talent and force of will alone, given the right circumstances.

To grasp the enormity of what he achieved in Barcelona, we also need to understand just how far behind Williams Ferrari was at the time. Schumacher qualified in third behind the Williams pairing of Damon Hill and Jacques Villeneuve, driving a lap he described as perfect – and yet he was still almost a full second off Hill's pole time. That he got as close as that was a minor miracle; team-mate Eddie Irvine's sixth place on the grid, achieved after extensive testing at the track, more accurately reflected the pace of the truculent, aerodynamically inexact Ferrari F310.

Such speed as the F310 did possess was delivered in traditional Ferrari fashion – by the engine. With rules reducing engine capacity to 3 litres, Ferrari had finally abandoned its V12s, which, turbo era aside, had served in its cars since 1966. The new V10 offered similar power to a V12 but with better torque and fuel consumption, thanks in part to lower frictional losses, and with the bonus of a shorter, stiffer construction. Schumacher, fresh out of a Benetton with a Renault V10 believed to be the best engine on the grid, had no complaints.

As for the car, Irvine dismissed it as 'almost undriveable', and even its creator, John Barnard, conceded it was not one of his better designs. Indeed, it and the F310 B update would be the last cars he'd design from his Guildford Technical Office, and the last Ferraris to date not designed and engineered in Maranello.

'SCHUMACHER QUALIFIED THIRD WITH A PERFECT LAP – YET HE WAS STILL ALMOST A FULL SECOND OFF HILL'S POLE TIME'

Clockwise from left
Watching Schumacher
scythe through the field
in the wet was all the more
impressive knowing that
the F310 was, in Eddie
Irvine's words 'almost
undriveable'; chasing
down the Williams of
Jacques Villeneuve;
blasting past Gerhard
Berger's Benetton.

'SCHUMACHER SEEMED
TO HAVE CHALLENGED
HIMSELF TO SHOW HE
WAS THE BEST DRIVER
IN THE BUSINESS'

'BY THE END OF THE SECOND LAP, ALMOST A THIRD OF THE FIELD HAD CRASHED OR SPUN OFF'

Rory Byrne and Ross Brawn replaced Barnard in 1997 and laid the groundwork for the five Drivers' and six Constructors' titles the Scuderia would win between 1999 and 2004.

Schumacher was so unsure of his chariot that in practice at the Spanish GP he tested two entirely different set-ups, with no sense of which might be right. It was already looking like it might be a very long weekend.

And then the drivers woke up on Sunday morning, looked out of their hotel windows and were greeted by an entirely different world to that in which they had qualified the day before. It wasn't just raining, it had been pouring for hours. The Circuit de Catalunya was soaked. Some would have gladly gone back to bed, but not, I suspect, Michael Schumacher. Always the hardest working driver in F1, he no doubt greeted his engineers with a spring in his step that morning. In racing there is no greater leveller than rain, and, when it rains, the true masters always come to the fore.

Moss was uncatchable in the rain, as was Jim Clark. At the 1968 German Grand Prix, held in a deluge, Jackie Stewart won the race and was out of the car and spectating before the next car came by four minutes later. Ayrton Senna was in a league of his own when he won his first Grand Prix at a wet Estoril in '85, and again when he won his last at Donington in '93. If Schumacher could just wrestle his way

through at the start and get the Williams drivers behind him, he had the skills to keep them there.

It was Helmuth von Moltke, a 19th-century head of the Prussian army, who said, 'No battle plan ever survives first contact with the enemy', and so it proved at Barcelona. Hill was slow away from pole, but unfortunately for Ferrari, Schumacher, troubled by a sticky clutch, was slower still. At the end of the first lap, having been passed by both Benettons, he was down in sixth place.

To give you some idea of the conditions, by the end of the second lap, six drivers – almost a third of the field – had crashed or spun off into retirement, including Irvine. Visibility was so bad that David Coulthard is still not sure which car he tangled with in the split-second before his race ended.

The only person who could see was Hill's team-mate, Jacques Villeneuve, and in a car designed by Adrian Newey on a circuit now legendary for the advantages it confers on cars with effective aerodynamics, he should have scampered away. But he didn't. And Schumacher wasn't letting his early setback put him off his stride.

He was further helped by Hill, who appeared completely unable to cope with the conditions and spun three times in seven laps, finally ending up in the wall and out of the race.

From top
The pit crew and the fans at the Circuit de Catalunya knew they had witnessed a performance for the ages; a sight that would become painfully familiar to Ferrari's rivals.

By the time of the first of these spins, Schumacher was already lining up Gerhard Berger's Benetton for third place. Five laps later he was past the other Benetton, driven by Jean Alesi, for second. And three laps after that he displaced Villeneuve from the lead.

Those who saw him thereafter saw a man in a race of his own. Having uncharacteristically binned his Ferrari at the previous Grand Prix in Monaco, Schumacher seemed to have challenged himself to show the world that he was the best driver in the business, and by such a margin that not even the most ardent fan of Hill or Villeneuve could argue.

Half the field was *hors de combat* before a third of the race was complete, and you could see most of those who remained go into survival mode. Just get to the finish, they thought, and there are be points to be had. And they were right, even at a time when points were only awarded to the top six cars – because that's how many made it to the end.

Schumacher took a different approach. Even then, relative speed in F1 was usually hard to see; a car going down the road at 180mph looks much the same as one doing 170mph. But you didn't need a stopwatch to tell that Schumacher was going faster than anyone else. It was no Prost-like exhibition of careful precision driving, either – indeed at times it looked as though someone of the finest Scandinavian rallying stock had slipped behind the wheel of the F310.

This was car control of a kind I'd not seen in F1 since the days before downforce made it

'BY HALF DISTANCE THE CAR WAS CLEARLY NOT FIRING ON ALL TEN, AND STILL THE GAP GREW'

more efficient to drive without a significant yaw angle. Yet here was Schumacher throwing his Ferrari around like it was a Mk2 Escort. In F1, gaps are measured in tenths, hundreds and occasionally thousandths of a second, but not this day. On certain laps he was three whole seconds quicker than anyone else on the track.

The most staggering thing about Schumacher's drive, though, is that he did it in a car that was not only uncooperative but sick as well. Early in the race his engine had sounded a little rough, but by half distance it was clearly not firing on all ten, and maybe not even nine, and still the gap grew. He pulled in for his second and final pit stop on the 42nd of 64 laps. When he rejoined – and remember how much slower pit stops were in those days, when cars were still refuelled mid-race – his closest rival was still over a minute behind.

Only then, with his point well and truly made, did Schumacher ease off the throttle and cruise to the finish, coming home 45 seconds ahead of Alesi and 48 seconds ahead of Villeneuve. Everyone else had been lapped.

Schumacher would win twice more that season, memorably at Spa and again at Monza in front of the adoring *Tifosi*, dragging Ferrari up to second place in the Constructors' Championship despite the painfully obvious flaws of the F310.

Of all Schumacher's victories, the 1996 Spanish GP is the one I remember most fondly. Not because it was his first for Ferrari, and not even because it was his best, because I don't feel in a position to make such a judgement. It's a race I love to think about because it's the one that convinced me he was not the pantomime villain that the Damon-loving British press had made him out to be. Yes, he had his failings and some of his driving was inexcusable, but at the Circuit de Catalunya that day I saw an F1 car being driven in a way I'd not seen since Senna's opening lap at Donington three years earlier.

This demonstration, though, lasted an entire race. By the end of it I was utterly convinced that Michael Schumacher was the best driver of the post-Senna era and, in the 25 years since 'The Reign in Spain', I have seen nothing to make me modify that view.

A MAN APART

Michael Schumacher was a hero to Ferrari fans, a villain to others. David Tremayne looks back at the career of a prodigiously gifted but polarising racer

Portrait Alamy

MICHAEL SCHUMACHER'S Formula 1 break came in Belgium in 1991 when Jordan's Bertrand Gachot was jailed for spraying a taxi driver with mace. Schumacher was so quick during a test at Silverstone that the team tried to slow him down after only four laps. But he was even more sensational when he got to Spa-Francorchamps, qualifying in seventh place. Listening in the debrief as Andrea de Cesaris explained that the Jordan felt very nervous in fifth gear through Blanchimont, he offered quietly: 'It feels much more comfortable if you keep it flat in sixth there.' Schuey had arrived.

He burned out the clutch at the start, then dumped Jordan for Benetton. Ayrton Senna, before he died at Imola in 1994, was convinced that the German's car was still running traction control, which had been outlawed the previous year. The subsequent discovery of the 'Option 13' launch control software in his Benetton's electronics did nothing to alleviate suspicions that something was amiss. And the manner in which he drove Damon Hill off the road in the season finale in Adelaide, clinching the title despite damaging his own car after making an unforced error and hitting a wall, cast him as Formula 1's new villain.

He dominated in 1995 in a Renault-engined Benetton, but his greatness really became clear when Jean Todt persuaded him to join Ferrari for 1996. Jean Alesi and Gerhard Berger had been quick, but Todt wanted the best. Things took a while to gel technically, but for the 1997 season Todt lured Rory Byrne and Ross Brawn from Benetton, and it became a matter of when rather than if Ferrari would return to the top of the sport.

Schumacher was a brilliant test driver. He was demanding yet hugely supportive, knew exactly what he wanted from his cars, and he always delivered on track. He was fit to a hitherto unknown level, too. Between 2000 and 2004, Ferrari was unbeatable. 'If God had wanted to create the perfect racing driver,' his manager Willi Weber declared, 'he'd have made him like Michael.'

There were countless moments of brilliance. he scored his first victory for Ferrari in 1996 in torrential rain, as recounted by Andrew Frankel (see page 182). In Hungary in 1998, Brawn told him he needed qualifying laps in the race to claw back 25 seconds in only 19 laps; he obliged, and won. Victory over McLaren's Mika Häkkinen at Suzuka in 2000 made him Ferrari's first World Champion since 1979. The following year in Malaysia he won despite an agonising 72-second pit stop, while in Austria in 2003 he won even after his Ferrari caught fire. The *Tifosi* revered him, and still do.

Brawn identified Schumacher's ability to adapt to different cars, tyres or conditions as a prime strength, allied to his fearsome speed – and a ruthless will to win. He lost the 1997 title after driving into Jacques Villeneuve in Jerez but coming off worse; the French-Canadian took the championship and Schumacher was disqualified. In 2006 he parked in Monaco's Rascasse corner, preventing Fernando Alonso, the man who succeeded him as champion, from taking pole for Renault.

There was no clearer illustration of his often indefensible win-at-all-costs mentality than the incident with former team-mate Rubens Barichello, whom Schumacher nearly squeezed into the pit wall in Hungary in 2010. 'It was a horrible move, the most dangerous I have ever gone through,' the Brazilian said afterwards.

'You get sympathy for free, but you have to earn envy,' Schumacher declared. 'Whoever comes second is always going to get more sympathy than the winner.'

'The drivers who criticise Michael aren't seven-time champions,' said Brawn. 'Successful people have to be uncompromising.'

Away from the track, though, Schumacher was different. This was the man who donated $10m to the victims of the 2004 Indian Ocean tsunami. That gesture provided an insight into his real persona, one we would have seen more frequently in retirement if not for his tragic skiing accident in 2013. ▣

More of the same?

The Roma is based on the relatively tame Portofino,
but it promises an entirely different driving experience.
John Barker heads to the Alps to find out if it can deliver

Photography Aston Parrott

't is *not* a Portofino with a fixed roof,' the chap from Ferrari tells us. 'Seventy per cent is new. It's a GT with a sporting edge.' We reserve judgement; we'll find out just what sort of car the Roma is shortly, on a day trip to the Alps. We'll be chasing up to the French border and the demanding roads of the Colle dell'Agnello.

Of one thing I'm already sure, though: the Roma is the most elegant production car from Ferrari in a decade, in styling a successor to models such as the 550 Maranello. To classic, fastback GT proportions, Ferrari has added a sharky nose with a version of the classic egg-crate grille. The rump is distinguished by its blade-like upper edge and four integrated tail-lights. The car has some excellent angles, and it's a dramatic sight when in motion, especially when it's approaching you head-on, the bands of daytime running lights seeming to lower the sharp nose, like the car means business.

The car breaks with current trends by hiding rather than showcasing the expertise of its maker in matters of aerodynamics; the upper surfaces are beautifully clean. Meanwhile, on the flat underfloor behind the front splitter are two curved deflectors – vortex generators – that direct the air towards the sills and help smooth the wake from the wheels, and at the rear there's a carbonfibre diffuser. The Roma's muscular haunches are like those of the Jaguar F-type and it employs a similar active rear spoiler solution: a flip-up wing that is stowed flush until needed, its deployment triggered by speed and the setting of the manettino dial.

I don't need to spend long with the car to realise it sounds good, too. As snapper Aston Parrott and I load our gear into the boot, there's another Roma idling next to ours, a sonorous burble spilling from its tailpipes. There are no silencers in the exhaust, sound absorption being handled by the gas particulate filters, and by playing with pipe lengths and diameters the engineers have achieved a purposeful voice similar to that of the F8 Tributo.

That boot isn't huge, being reasonably long and wide but rather low, though the backrests of the teeny rear seats fold down to make a sort of parcel shelf. Dropping into the Roma is like lowering yourself into the bath, the individual driver and passenger cockpit areas giving an close, intimate feel.

Rolling away, the steering feels a little light, but I won't give it another thought all day, a sure sign that it's very well judged. It responds to the smallest inputs, but it's not jumpy, not overly bright.

The first clue that the Roma is going to be a bit special in use comes within yards of setting off. We start in Comfort mode – the others available being Wet, Sport, Race and ESC Off – and on leaving the grounds of the hotel we find ourselves on cobbled streets, but all that comes through is a soft, quiet pattering. A little further on there's some unavoidable and horribly broken asphalt, which is also negotiated with remarkably little fuss. But don't go thinking that the Roma is some lazy GT with a chassis made of blancmange. The ride quality is a result of superb wheel control and comes *with* dynamic precision, rather than at the expense of it.

Oddly, there's little perceptible difference switching to Sport or Race, no firming of the ride, no uplift in steering weight, though the gearshifts are a bit crisper and keener. I'm not bothered, because the Roma already feels as responsive and controlled and precise as I want. We'll get to ESC Off later.

At the first opportunity to give the throttle a decent squeeze, the Roma picks up crisply and drives forward with all the thrilling eagerness you expect from a 600bhp Ferrari – something that couldn't be said of the Portofino. Sure, the Roma is hauling nearly 100kg less than the Portofino, has 19bhp more, and the gearing of its lower ratios is around four per cent shorter, but the difference in performance feel between the two cars is too dramatic to be attributed to those things alone.

After less than 20 minutes in the car, then, any scepticism I was harbouring is gone: you'd never guess that the Roma shares *anything* with the Portofino, except maybe its 3.9-litre twin-turbo V8, though even that feels completely different in character here.

L4 14755

2020 Ferrari Roma

Engine 3855cc twin-turbo V8 **Power** 611bhp @ 5750-7500rpm
Torque 560lb ft @ 3000-5250rpm **Transmission** Eight-speed semi-automatic DCT,
rear-wheel drive **Steering** Rack and pinion, electrically assisted **Suspension** Front and rear:
double wishbones, coil springs, adaptive dampers, anti-roll bar **Brakes** Carbon-ceramic discs
Weight 1570kg **0-62mph** 3.4sec (claimed) **Top speed** 199mph (claimed)

The flat-plane-crank engine is mid-front mounted (its front face is wholly behind the front axle line) and thanks to some fettling it makes 611bhp between 5750 and 7000rpm. The car shares the wheelbase of the Portofino, but the Roma has different proportions and dimensions. It's 70mm longer, 36mm wider and 17mm lower, and has wider wheel tracks too – greater by 19mm at the front and 36mm at the rear. The 20in wheels are the same size as the Portofino's. The lack of a folding hardtop is the biggest reason why the Roma is 94kg lighter and has a near 50:50 static weight distribution. The figures for the tail-heavy Portofino are 46:54, and that's without the hardtop retracted. Given that the Portofino only feels 600bhp strong (or 592bhp strong, to be precise) at its top end, it's no wonder that it resists oversteer. The Roma promises to be different.

I suspect that the most contentious part of the Roma will prove to be its switchgear, if that's the right word here, which is mostly shared with the SF90 Stradale (see page 200). There's a wide TFT (thin-film transistor) screen with a central tacho and different displays either side, and many touch-sensitive switch pads – some of which revert to black when not in use. There's also a tablet-like central touchscreen set into the dashboard.

If you want to be able to adjust the audio volume or the cabin temperature or do almost anything else once you're driving, you'll need to spend some time practising before you set off, and certain functions may still elude you. This level of electronic sophistication might feel appropriate in the SF90 Stradle, a 1000bhp hybrid, but in a relatively simple front-engined, rear-drive GT, it feels like overkill. Perhaps the greatest crime is that the start-stop button is no longer a physical button. At least the manettino switch still has its little flipper.

Even while the car is stationary the gizmos cause me some bother. We stop for Aston to take some photographs and I stay put while he sets up a shot. Every time he returns to the car he's been locked out, and I have to lean over to open his door as I'm unable to find the central locking button. By chance, we discover that it is roof-mounted (yes, really) and touch-sensitive, and while there's a loud confirmation click for certain button pushes, there isn't one for unlocking the doors, so you don't know if you have or not. And while we're on the doors, there's no internal latch; instead you press a button on the door pull.

Happily, it's easy to put all this aside, because the further you drive the Roma, the more impressive it gets. Refinement is good, the seats will still be comfortable after a long day at the wheel, and the view is pretty special too: the bonnet bulge and the way the front wings rise to help judge the car's width are reminiscent of the aforementioned 550 Maranello.

Stretch the V8 and the pace never lets up, the rev-counter needle swinging to 7500rpm and the eight-speed DCT slipping instantly into the next ratio so that the acceleration is seamless and relentless. It's a fast car, the Roma, and its exhaust note has real presence. Pedestrians swivel to see what's coming and they all smile when they clock the car. Not just Italians, either: when we park at the summit of the Colle dell'Agnello with a view of Italy on one side and France on the other, tourists of many nationalities ask for selfies with the Roma.

'Pedestrians swivel at the sound, and they all smile when they clock the Roma'

The ease with which it deals with these mountain roads and their difficult, weather-beaten surfaces suggests that the car will feel right at home on some of our favourite roads back in the UK – but only with the Pirelli P Zero that was developed especially for the chassis. The alternative tyre is the Michelin Pilot Sport 4 S, and although it offers similar steering quality and grip, the ride is much tougher. There was no need to use the 'bumpy road' button at all on the Pirelli, but it gets a lot of use when we try the Michelin.

The Roma feels naturally agile and there's appreciably less roll than in the Portofino. Development driver Raffaele de Simone says there's not one thing alone that makes the Roma steer more directly. It uses the same physical steering components as the Portofino but the structure of the Roma is stiffer, while the mounting of its rear axle is more positive and so there's no slack to take up; you turn the wheel and the whole car turns. I reckon the slim steering wheel rim enhances feel, too.

Above from left
The 3855cc twin-turbo V8 produces 611bhp; the Roma is a comfortable place to be on long drives, as long as you choose the right tyre; the electronic switchgear is clever, but annoyingly fiddly at times.

I'm sure that if we'd got time at the Fiorano track, the Roma would have impressed with its poise, because even scratching around here on narrow switchbacks it feels properly handy – responsive, balanced and grippy. Drive it to the limit of front grip, if you dare, and you'll be flying, occasionally leaning heavily on the powerful carbon-ceramic brakes. Get on the power early to give the rear its share of the workload and traction control quietly asserts itself, releasing the torque only once the car is pretty much straight and the traction is undefeatable.

Flick the manettino to ESC Off and you appreciate just how much grip there is and how hard the electronic differential works to maintain traction. Even once you've turned in sharply to a hairpin, it takes a proper slug of throttle to unstick the rear. Once it's out there, the Roma feels comfortable with a twist of opposite lock and comes back into line neatly, and it's much the same in the wet, too. It's a very impressive car – and definitely not a fixed-head Portofino.

The Portofino (née California) has always struck me as the car Ferrari feels it has to offer to bring in a new audience, and I reckon it was a difficult car to build, because it needed to look, sound and feel like a Ferrari but be docile enough for any customer.

The sharp-suited Roma was developed with no such constraints. Imagine the F8 Tributo remade as a front-engine, rear-drive coupé and you're pretty much on the money. Yet while it's dynamic and fast and sporty, it delivers against the GT bit of the brief as well. Yes, it would be awesome with a 600bhp V12, making it a true 550 Maranello successor, but the Roma is a fabulous Ferrari in its own right, and first-time buyers couldn't hope for a better introduction to the marque. *End*

LIKE A HURRICANE

With almost 1000bhp available
from its petrol and electric motors,
the SF90 Stradale is a force of nature

Words Mike Duff   **Photography** Ferrari

Above and right
The RAC-e transmission is for the two electric motors mounted at the front. There's a third at the rear, and together they can make up to 217bhp; but the main motive force comes from the latest version of the F154 twin-turbocharged V8, which produces an astonishing 769bhp.

How quickly the supercar game moves on. It feels like it was only yesterday that Ferrari launched the LaFerrari – a car definitive enough to earn the definite article – and yet here we are with another Ferrari hybrid that is more powerful, faster, quicker around Fiorano, and much easier to drive.

It is inevitable that parallels will be drawn between the two cars, but the differences need to be scrupulously observed. The LaFerrari is one of Ferrari's 'special' cars, the limited editions that only the brand's best friends and most loyal customers stand a chance of being allowed to purchase. The SF90, on the other hand, is a regular production model available to mere mortals, and it comes with no defined production limit and a price tag that, in most parts of the world, is less than half that of its illustrious predecessor.

The biggest difference is also the most obvious: the SF90, while a handsome car, lacks the visual drama that Ferrari seems to reserve for its true range-toppers. It looks slightly tame when compared to a LaFerrari, or the strange, ugly beauty of the Enzo. But the SF's wind-tunnel-sculpted aerodynamics allow it to combine impressively low drag with the ability to make up to 390kg of downforce, with a clever 'shut-off Gurney flap' on the rear deck that falls to reveal a more aggressive wing element when required. As a piece of engineering, the SF90 is a tour de force, and more than that, a declaration of war – a hugely complex hybrid that is years ahead of what we know rivals are working on.

The petrol side of the powertrain is the easy part to explain: a 4-litre V8 based on the F154 engine fitted to the F8 Tributo, but with a redesigned cylinder head, new turbos and higher injection pressures. It makes 769bhp – 59bhp more than the F8 – but weighs 25kg less. The V8 blends its efforts with those of three electric motors. Two of these are at the front, driving one wheel each but sitting within a combined transmission dubbed RAC-e and capable of torque vectoring. The third is a state-of-the-art 'axial flux' motor sandwiched between the combustion engine and the eight-speed, twin-clutch gearbox. The electric motors can add up to 217bhp of power, that figure dictated by the peak flow of the 8kW/h lithium-ion battery rather than hardware limitations. When the front electric motors disengage at speeds above 130mph, the rear motor is then able to absorb the full 162kW current, keeping total output the same.

As with mainstream plug-in hybrids, the SF90 is able to drive under pure electric power, which is done using the front pair of motors. Driving this way feels deeply strange. Acceleration in eMode is limited – subjectively it feels a little less sprightly than the latest Nissan Leaf – but it is the almost total silence that is oddest. When Enzo Ferrari famously said, 'I build engines and attach wheels to them', this is certainly not what he had in mind. Ferrari claims an EV range of up to 15 miles, with the electric mode working at speeds of up to 84mph. The company reckons the feature will be popular with owners wanting to sneak out for an early blast without waking the family or the neighbours. It's also why there's no mechanical reverse, the SF90 always backing up on electric power.

'Even using little more than half throttle, the Stradale feels quicker than many bona fide supercars'

You'll be unsurprised to hear that I don't experience the SF90's silent running for very long. After starting in Hybrid mode by default, any move to make faster progress will soon fire the V8 into raucous life; alternatively this can be done by selecting either the Performance or Qualify modes using the 'e-Manettino' buttons on the left of the steering wheel. Doing this immediately turns the SF90 into a proper Ferrari, with performance and a soundtrack to match, the engine snarling and savage as the red line at 8000rpm is approached.

Although there is little evidence of the electric assistance under hard use, it is still there – and usually doing more than just adding to the huge longitudinal g-forces the powertrain can generate. Most obviously, sending drive to the front wheels both increases traction and also allows the system to use power to pull the car out of any hydrocarbon-induced slip at the back. So while the acceleration figures – 2.5sec for 0-62mph and 6.7sec for 0-124mph – are astonishing, it's the SF90's ability to find traction that's more impressive.

The electrical torque-vectoring at the front is almost invisible. Only on the twistiest roads above Maranello is there any sensation of power being shared between the steered wheels, and even then only in the very tightest corners. The motors also allow what is effectively an electric form of traction control, managing slip by increasing the rate at which energy is being harvested rather than reining in the engine. The system also allows for high levels of regenerative braking, the need to combine this with friction retardation from the carbon-ceramic discs requiring a brake-by-wire system. Initially this set-up seems odd, with a very short pedal stroke and only gentle pressure needed to produce reasonably strong forces, but it feels more natural as forces increase, and two hours in I was fully acclimatised.

The eight-speed, twin-clutch transmission is, amazingly, even quicker and more decisive than Ferrari's lightning-fast seven-speeder. The big problem with driving the SF90 on the road is one of frustration. Despite its ability to find grip, the real world offers few opportunities to fully unleash it, and getting the accelerator pedal to the end of its long travel is something that will only be done rarely and very briefly. Even short-shifting and using little more than half throttle, the Stradale feels quicker than many bona fide supercars.

And yet the suspension is impressively compliant and the ride quality surprisingly plush with the (conventional) manettino in the Sport setting. There is also the ability to soften the adaptive dampers further with a 'bumpy road' setting. The SF90 is around 120kg heavier than the F8, but

Clockwise from left
The cabin is beautifully finished and a clear step up from that of most 'regular' modern Ferraris. The steering wheel features the usual manettino plus a new 'e-Manettino'; chances to explore the SF90's performance on the the road are few and far between, but Fiorano gives a glimpse of its true potential.

its mass is kept under impressively tight control, with no bottoming-out even over the sort of dips and compressions that have me braced for the sound of carbon on tarmac.

A gentler run back to Maranello gives me the chance to better appreciate the cabin. The SF90 is a comfortable cruiser and surprisingly hushed in gentle use, even with the engine running. Most functions are now initiated through touch-sensitive panels, with data relayed to a single, 16-inch screen ahead of the driver that also contains the instrument displays. It does work well, although the system plays a curious 'page turning' noise when you swipe between screens. There are a few ergonomic grumbles: the top of the dashboard throws up nasty reflections in the windscreen and the fan is noisy when working to keep the cabin cool in 30-degree weather. But these are small niggles.

After lunch at the famous Montana restaurant, sitting beneath race overalls once worn by Michael Schumacher and Rubens Barrichello, it's time for the next part of the traditional Ferrari launch: the chance to experience the car on the track at Fiorano, and to regret eating so much pasta.

2020 Ferrari SF90 Stradale

Engine 3990cc twin-turbo V8, plus three electric motors
Power 986bhp: 769bhp @ 7500rpm (V8) plus 217bhp (hybrid system)
Torque 590lb ft @ 6000rpm (V8) **Transmission** Eight-speed semi-automatic DCT,
four-wheel drive **Steering** Rack and pinion, electrically assisted **Suspension** Front:
double wishbones, coil springs, adaptive dampers, anti-roll bar. Rear: multi-link, coil springs,
adaptive dampers, anti-roll bar **Brakes** Carbon-ceramic discs **Weight** 1600kg
0-62mph 2.5sec (claimed) **Top speed** 211mph (claimed)

COVID restrictions mean nobody is allowed in the cockpit with me, so I'm sent out alone, with the near-impossible task of sticking with factory test driver Fabrizio Toschi, who is driving a prototype still in its disguise wrap. I turn the e-Manettino to the Qualify setting to ensure the powertrain is giving its all, and twist the normal manettino to an angle corresponding with Race.

Most cars feel slower on a track, but the SF90 manages to feel even quicker because here you can enjoy the full brutality of the car's acceleration; Fiorano's straights seem far shorter than I remember from my last visit.

But the big surprise is discovering how oversteery the car feels on track, with some yaw angles that feel impressively liberal for the sort of machine-curated slides I presume I'm experiencing. It's only after a lap of this that I look down and discover the manettino is actually pointing to 'TC off', and that I've discovered the SF90 is far friendlier on the limit than any near-1000bhp Ferrari has the right to be.

Switching to Race imposes more discipline, and although the organ-sloshing acceleration remains, the way the car turns into corners and hooks up seemingly impossible traction on the way out is even more astonishing. I still don't catch up with Toschi, though.

Ferrari didn't intend for the track to be the SF90's natural environment, something made clear by that Stradale suffix, but only under the hardest braking was there any sense of the extra mass of the hybrid system. And despite carrying more weight than the LaFerrari, the regular SF90 is an impressive 0.3sec quicker around a lap of Fiorano – with the optional Assetto Fiorano handling pack giving a whole one-second advantage.

I come away from a day with the SF90 Stradale thinking of Moore's Law – the principle, established by Intel's co-founder, that the power of a microchip would double over a two-year period. Something similar seems to happen with ultra-high-performance hybrids and, although I'm not supposed to compare them, the SF90 is a much more technically accomplished car than the LaFerrari was. When it comes to using electrification to add excitement, rather than virtuousness, Ferrari is leading the pack. *End*

207

BADGE OF HONOUR

Delwyn Mallett delves into the history of
Ferrari's iconic *Cavallino Rampante* emblem

WHILE ON A strafing mission against Austrian forces in June 1918, Italian fighter pilot Count Francesco Baracca crashed fatally on Montello hill in the province of Treviso. The fuselage of his biplane bore the *Cavallino Rampante* (Italian for 'prancing horse'), his personal emblem and that of the squadron he commanded. There is some confusion surrounding his death. The Italians believe he was brought down by ground fire, but there is support for the Austrian version of events – that he was shot down by one of their fighters. When the crash site was reached three days later by Italian forces, Baracca's body was recovered and taken to his birthplace for an emotional funeral. More than a century later his emblem is one of the most recognisable logos in the world, propelled to that position by another great Italian merchant of speed: Enzo Ferrari.

It is difficult to overstate the importance of motor racing in Italy in the early years of the 20th century. It was embraced by the wealthy and the proletariat alike, and was also promoted by intellectuals, poets and artists. Nuvolari's tortoise mascot was given to him by the poet, soldier and proto-fascist Gabriele D'Annunzio – one of Enzo's favourite writers, incidentally. The machine and speed, in particular as represented by the aeroplane and the car, became symbolic of Italy's progress from an agrarian economy to a modern industrial state.

Baracca, a decade older than Enzo, was born in 1888 in Lugo di Romagna. At the age of 19 he enrolled in the military academy in Modena, and as a keen equestrian he soon became a sub-lieutenant in the Royal Piedmont Cavalry, whose emblem was a prancing horse. Like many young men of the era, Baracca was fascinated by aeroplanes and, after learning to fly in France in 1912, he became a pilot in the Italian Air Force. Italy entered World War One in 1915, joining the Allied Powers and fighting against Austro-Hungarian forces in appallingly difficult mountainous terrain along the Italian-Austrian border.

Baracca scored Italy's first aerial victory of the war in April 1916, while flying a Nieuport 11, and a string of further triumphs – always in craft decorated with the mark of his old cavalry regiment – saw him become a national hero. By the time of his death, Baracca's tally was 34 and he was revered as Italy's 'ace of aces'.

Enzo was conscripted in 1917, but rather than being sent to the front with a gun, he was given the job of shoeing mules. Perhaps, given that the name 'Ferrari' is etymologically close to 'blacksmith', some military official felt it was a good gag. As mentioned elsewhere in this publication, Enzo lost his father and brother to the flu during the war, and he nearly succumbed himself before being invalided out of the army in 1918. After recuperating, in 1919 he found work with Costruzioni Meccaniche Nazionali in Milan, and he soon fulfilled his ambition

Opposite and below
Fighter pilot Count Francesco Baracca with his SPAD S.XIII, around 1918. He and his biplane would soon meet their end, but his prancing horse emblem lived on and returned to prominence after World War One when Scuderia Ferrari cars began winning races.

to become a racer. Driving a CMN, he was classified ninth in the Targa Florio, and when he returned to the great road race in 1920, then an employee of Alfa Romeo, he came second.

He took the reins of Baracca's prancing horse in June 1923 after winning at the Circuito del Savio. He was congratulated by Baracca's father, Count Enrico, and later on Baracca's mother, Countess Paolina, suggested that Enzo use her son's prancing horse on his car as 'it will bring you good luck'. A cynic might say that it had not brought her son luck, and Enzo did not take up the offer immediately – though this was almost certainly because in the same year, after Ugo Sivocci's quadrifoglio-adorned car won the Targa Florio, Alfa Romeo adopted the four-leaf clover emblem for its team cars.

In 1924, ahead of what would have been his most important race to date, the Grand Prix de l'ACF in Lyon, Enzo had a crisis of confidence and pulled out. For the next few years he appeared only intermittently behind the wheel while focusing on building his business as an Alfa distributor from his new base in Modena. Then, in 1929, at a dinner of motorsport enthusiasts, he had the idea that would set him on his way to fame: he proposed to start a 'racing club' to prepare cars for wealthy clients who wanted to go racing without getting their hands dirty. The Società Anonima Scuderia Ferrari was registered on 1 December 1929.

'By the time of his death, Baracca was revered as Italy's "ace of aces" and had racked up 34 aerial victories'

The Ferrari version of the prancing horse made its first appearance on the new company's notepaper and on the masthead of the in-house periodical, *La Scuderia Ferrari*. The magazine allowed Enzo to indulge one of his interests; he had considered becoming a journalist (or an opera singer) at one time.

Alfa Romeo, which was publicly owned and under financial pressure, decided to outsource its racing activities and use Scuderia Ferrari as its de facto factory team. The first car to wear the Cavallino Rampante was the Ferrari Alfa 8C 2300 that won the Spa 24 hours in 1932.

Enzo effected a number of 'improvements' to the horse, however. Baracca's lucky charm had both hind legs on the ground, and an extravagant tail pointing downwards. Enzo's version was more *rampante*, balanced on one leg with a slimmed-down tail flicking saucily upwards. On his racing Alfas, the horse sat in a shield of yellow (the official colour of Modena) topped by the Italian tricolour in a thin chevron stripe and the letters S and F, for Scuderia Ferrari, in a cursive script either side of the horse's grounded leg.

In 1938 Alfa took its racing team back in-house, creating Alfa Corse. Enzo returned to Milan, but only briefly. In November 1939, unwilling to be a mere employee, he left Alfa and decamped back to Modena. Having agreed with Alfa Romeo that he would not produce cars under his own name for four years, he rebranded as Auto Avio Costruzioni, and in 1943 he relocated again, to Maranello.

The first car to carry the maestro's name and the now-familiar rectangular bonnet badge took shape during 1946 and made its debut in 1947 at Piacenza circuit. The chunky little 1500cc V12 Ferrari 125 (125cc per cylinder) was leading the 30-lap race with only three to go when a fuel pump failure brought it to a halt. Two weeks later, however, the 125 was victorious in the Grand Prix of Rome and a legend was born.

In 1952, to differentiate his race entries
from the increasing number of customer cars
on the circuits, Enzo reintroduced the shield
that he'd last used on his Scuderia cars in
the 1930s. The prancing horse has also featured
as a stand-alone symbol on radiator or engine
grilles since 1959. It has been redrawn several
times over the years, though few Ferrari fans
will have been aware of any change. Even the
2002 alteration, which saw the horse transform
from a stallion into a mare, went largely
unnoticed, despite the fact that the Ferrari logo
was by then pretty much ubiquitous.

The dynamics of the luxury goods market
changed fundamentally during the 1970s and
'80s, when conspicuous consumption came to
be viewed by many as a virtue rather than a
vice. Consumers began to define themselves by
the things they bought. Brands such as Ralph
Lauren ensured that their garments would be
recognised instantly by strategically positioning
a logo (in Lauren's case, as it happens, another
horse) where it could not be missed.

Porsche watches, sunglasses and accessories
heralded the arrival of an era in which motor
manufacturers became 'luxury lifestyle' brands.
It should be noted, though, that for many years
the only way to acquire a prancing horse badge
was to buy the car it was attached to – unless
the Old Man himself favoured you with a
presentation watch.

Today you'll find the Cavallino Rampante
plastered, with Ferrari's blessing, on a vast array

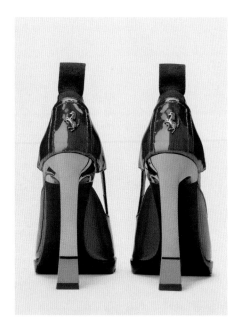

of products from headphones to high heels.
I suspect Enzo would not have approved.
He dressed soberly and once declared that his
philosophy as a manufacturer was to maintain
exclusivity by 'building one less car than the
market wanted'.

Not long after Enzo had sold his company
to Fiat, he received the motoring journalist
Griffith Borgeson in his private office.
Borgeson noted that the room was almost
empty, containing a simple desk and three
chairs. The walls were almost empty, too,
bearing only a large photograph of Enzo's wife,
Laura; a painting of a speeding, red racing car;
and a large colour print of Francesco Baracca
standing beside his SPAD fighter. *End*

KEYSTONE / HULTON ARCHIVE / GETTY IMAGES

HERD MENTALITY

*Ferrari is just one of many
companies to adopt the
horse as its emblem…*

Mobil, then 'The Vacuum Oil Company',
patented its wonderful Pegasus logo
in 1911, although it didn't become
a familiar sight on racing cars until
the 1940s. Interestingly, Ferrari's
Indianapolis 500 entry in 1952
carried the 'flying horse' as well
as its own prancing horse.

The cars built by one of Ferrari's
greatest rivals also sport a prancing
horse. Not long after Porsche had
started production of the 356, so the
story goes, the marque's US importer,
Max Hoffman, suggested that the car
should carry a badge. Ferry Porsche
did a rough sketch based on the
crests of Baden-Württemberg and
its capital, Stuttgart. The crest of
the latter just happens to be a
prancing horse on a yellow field.

From 1956 to 1961 another iconic
Italian marque, Ducati, also used the
Cavallino Rampante on the fairings
of its desmodromic-valved racing
motorcycles. Fabio Taglioni, Ducati's
renowned designer, was born in the
same town as Francesco Baracca and
his father had been a World War One
pilot, though not in Baracca's squadron.
Taglioni, who counted Enzo as a friend,
obtained permission from Ferrari to use
its version of the prancing horse.

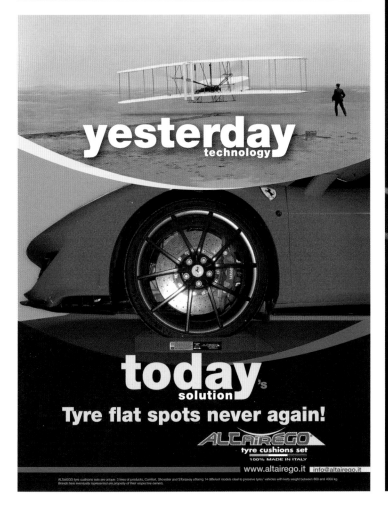

166 // 195 // 212
(1947-1951)

First true road car was 166, with 2-litre Colombo V12 (166 the capacity of each cylinder). Larger-engined 195 and 212 followed. Total built c200.
166 Inter: 1995cc V12, 110bhp, 106mph

340 // 342 // 375 America
(1950-53)

Based on evolution of 166 chassis, America series used 'long-block' Lampredi V12 of 4.1 and later 4.5 litres. Just 41 built, all highly prized today.
340 America: 4102cc V12, 200bhp, 140mph

250 Europa
(1953-55)

Ferrari's first real GT car and first to carry the 250 series nomenclature, though power was from a short-block version of Lampredi V12. Just 17 built.
250 Europa: 2963cc V12, 200bhp, 140mph

250 GT Boano // Ellena
(1955-59)

First 'volume-produced' Ferrari with classic 3-litre Colombo V12. Most designed by Pinin Farina, but built by Boano and later Ellena. Total built: 130.
250 GT: 2953cc V12, 240bhp, 125mph

250 GT 'Tour de France'
(1956-59)

A special 250 GT named for Ferrari's win in the Tour de France race, built by Scaglietti with a tuned Colombo V12. One of the all-time greats.
250 GT TdF: 2953cc V12, 260bhp, 137mph

410 Superamerica
(1955-59)

Replacement for the 375 America, with the big Lampredi V12 now up to 5 litres. Just 38 built in three series, fabulously expensive when new.
410 Superamerica: 4963cc V12, 340bhp, 150mph

250 GT Cabriolet
(1956-1962)

Less sporting than the Spyders of the period, the Cabriolets were fine touring cars. Series 2 (above) arrived in 1960. Around 240 built in total.
Cabriolet Series 2: 2953cc V12, 240bhp, 130mph

250 California Spyder LWB
(1957-59)

Charismatic, competition-derived two-seater roadster with tuned engine from Tour de France, designed for US market. Only 50 were made.
Cali Spyder LWB: 2953cc V12, 240bhp, 137mph

250 GT Coupé Pinin Farina
(1958-1960)

Staple late-'50s Ferrari was a clean-lined, two-seat coupé designed and built by Pinin Farina. Total production run of c 350 was Ferrari's biggest yet.
250 GT Coupé PF: 2953cc V12, 240bhp, 130mph

250 GT SWB **(1959-1962)**

The SWB, or Short Wheelbase Berlinetta, is one of the greatest and most collectable of all Ferraris. Around half of the 167 built were competition cars, raced with much success, including by Stirling Moss, but the SWB was equally brilliant on road. Shortened wheelbase meant extra agility, 280bhp version of 3-litre Colombo V12 gave 160mph+ performance, Pinin Farina lines are sublime.
250 GT SWB: 2953cc V12, 280bhp, 165mph

250 California Spyder SWB
(1959-1961)

Based on 250 GT SWB chassis and engine, the new Spyder was even more desirable than the original. Just 55 built and hugely valuable today.
Cali Spyder SWB: 2953cc V12, 280bhp, 140mph

250 GT/E 2+2
(1960-63)

First four-seater production Ferrari used 3-litre V12 from the berlinetta, though heavier body blunted performance. Sold well, though – 955 in total.
GT/E 2+2: 2953cc V12, 240bhp, 136mph

400 Superamerica
(1960-64)

Targeted at the US, the '400' in this case referred to the 4-litre version of the Lampredi V12. Aimed at the super-rich, only around 50 were built.
400 Superamerica: 3967cc V12, 340bhp, 160mph

250 GTO
(1962-64)

A racer, though some were road-registered, GTO was ultimate evolution of the 250 berlinetta. Just 39 made, each today worth £40m-plus.
250 GTO: 2953cc V12, 300bhp, 175mph

250 GT Berlinetta Lusso
(1962-64)

Last of the 250 line and one of the most beautiful of all Ferraris. Based on 250 GTO chassis and used a detuned version of the GTO's engine.
250 Lusso: 2953cc V12, 250bhp, 149mph

330 America // 330 GT 2+2
(1963-67)

330 America based on 250 GT/E 2+2 but with new 4-litre V12. Replaced in 1964 by restyled 330 GT 2+2 (above), of which 1099 were produced.
330 GT: 3967cc V12, 300bhp, 152mph

500 Superfast
(1964-66)

Evolved from 400 Superamerica with a mighty, 5-litre version of Lampredi V12 and plush cabin. Aimed at playboys and royalty, just 37 were built.
500 Superfast: 4963cc V12, 394bhp, 174mph

275 GTB // GTB/4 **(1964-68)**

Replacement for the 250 series of berlinettas, the 275 GTB introduced all-independent suspension, disc brakes all round and a five-speed transaxle, together with a new, 3.3-litre version of the Colombo V12, which made 275bhp in basic form or 300bhp in four-cam GTB/4 form. Production of all versions reached 970. One of the great Ferrari road cars and highly coveted today, especially in alloy body form.
275 GTB/4: 3286cc V12, 300bhp, 165mph

275 GTS
(1964-66)

275 roadster shared underpinnings of 275 GTB, including 3.3-litre V12, but little else, with totally different – but still appealing – Pininfarina styling.
275 GTS: 3286cc V12, 275bhp, 140mph

330 GTC // GTS
(1966-68)

Two-seater coupé and spyder variants on the 330 theme with the same 4-litre V12. GTC is far more common with 300 built compared with 100 GTSs.
330 GTC: 3967cc V12, 300bhp, 152mph

365 California
(1966-67)

First 365 model featuring new, 4.4-litre V12. Replaced the 500 Superfast as the flagship car. Similarly expensive and rare, with only 14 sold.
365 California: 4390cc V12, 320bhp, 152mph

275 NART Spyder
(1966-68)

Created for US dealer Luigi Chinetti (NART from his North American Racing Team). Just ten built, making this among most valuable of all Ferraris.
NART Spyder: 3286cc V12, 300bhp, 155mph

365 GT 2+2
(1968-1970)

Replacement for the 330 GT 2+2, the vast 365 GT had the new 4.4-litre V12 and was the first Ferrari 2+2 with independent rear suspension. 800 built.
365 GT: 4390cc V12, 320bhp, 150mph

Dino 206 GT (1968-69)

Launched as a 'sub brand' and not actually badged as a Ferrari, the Dino broke with tradition by having a V6 rather than a V12 and placing it behind rather than in front of the driver. The 2-litre V6 didn't really have the power to match the Pininfarina lines and the 206 was replaced by the torquier 2.4-litre 246 GT after just 153 had been built. Still a landmark car.
206 GT: 1987cc V6, 180bhp, 140mph

365 GTC // GTS
(1968-1970)

Essentially the 330 GTC and GTS with the bigger, 4.4-litre engine, 150 coupés were built, but just 15 spyders, which makes them sought-after today.
365 GTC: 4390cc V12, 320bhp, 152mph

365 GTB/4 // GTS/4
(1968-1974)

Replacement for the 275 GTB/4, the mighty Daytona had highly tuned 4.4-litre Colombo V12 and hit a true 174mph. 1284 berlinettas but just 122 spyders built.
365 GTB/4: 4390cc V12, 352bhp, 174mph

Dino 246 GT // GTS
(1969-1974)

Steel rather than alloy body of 206, but 246 was still usefully quicker. Targa-roofed GTS arrived in 1972. A big commercial hit, with total of 3761 sold.
246 GT: 2418cc V6, 195bhp, 146mph

365 GTC/4
(1971-72)

Softer 2+2 coupé derivative of Daytona with detuned engine, power steering, etc. In many ways nicer to drive. Sold 500 in just 18 months.
365 GTC/4: 4390cc V12, 340bhp, 163mph

365 GT4 2+2 // 400 GT // 400i // 412 GT (1972-1989)

Long-lived series of four-seaters, mostly autos, these are big, slightly soft and extremely thirsty, but rather handsome saloons. Total built: 2907.
412 GT: 4944cc V12, 340bhp, 155mph

365 GT4 Berlinetta Boxer // 512 BB // 512 BBi (1973-1985)

Replacement for the Daytona, the BB was Ferrari's first mid-engined supercar. Power was from a new 4.4-litre (later 5-litre) flat-12 engine. Total built: 2323.
BB 512i: 4942cc V12, 360bhp, 188mph

308 GT4 2+2
(1973-1980)

Originally badged as a Dino, the 308 GT4 2+2, with two tiny rear seats, was styled by Bertone rather than Pininfarina and had Ferrari's first V8. Total built: 2826.
308 GT4: 2926cc V8, 251bhp, 147mph

308 GTB // GTS // QV
(1975-1985)

Same V8 as the 308 GT4, but Ferrari returned to Pininfarina for the GTB. Targa-roofed GTS and 32v QV followed. Huge success, with over 12,000 sold in all.
308 GTB: 2926cc V8, 251bhp, 152mph

Mondial 8 // QV // QV Cabriolet // 3.2 // T (1980-1994)

Replaced the 308 GT4 2+2. Variants included 32v QV, cabriolet and the T, which saw the V8 turned from transverse to longitudinal. Over 6000 sold in all.
Mondial 3.2: 3185cc V8, 270bhp, 158mph

288 GTO
(1984-87)

Homologation special for Group B racing, GTO used fierce twin-turbo 2.9-litre version of 308 V8. Only 272 built, and they're worth a fortune today.
288 GTO: 2855cc tt V8, 394bhp, 188mph

Testarossa // 512 TR // F512 M
(1984-1996)

Testarossa ('redhead') replaced BB as mainstream flagship, adding extra usability. 512 TR and F512 M upped power. Total of all variants almost 10,000.
F512 M: 4943cc flat-12, 440bhp, 196mph

328 GTB // GTS
(1985-88)

Minor tweaks to the winning formula of the 308, with a small increase in capacity to 3.2 litres providing more power and torque. Another 7412 units sold.
328 GTB: 3185cc V8, 270bhp, 163mph

F40 **(1987-1992)**

Developed from the 288 GTO but with even more extensive use of carbonfibre and Kevlar in construction, the F40 was the first Ferrari to boast a 200mph-plus top speed, and the last Ferrari developed and approved for production during Enzo's lifetime. It was effectively a race car for the road and collectors and investors loved it: 1315 were built.
F40: 2936cc tt V8, 478bhp, 201mph

348 TB // TS // Speciale // GTB // GTS // Spider **(1989-1995)**

328 replacement saw V8 upped to 3.4 litres and turned lengthways, while body featured TR-style side-slats. On-limit handling tricky, but it sold well: 8844 in all.
348 GTB: 3405cc V8, 300bhp, 170mph

456 GT // 456M GT
(1993-2004)

Replacement for the 412, the 456 had an all-new 5.5-litre V12 up front and 2+2 seating. Updated M (for *modificata*) from 1998. Total built: 3289.
456 GT: 5472cc V12, 436bhp, 186mph

F355 Berlinetta // GTS // Spider
(1994-99)

Prettier, faster and better-handling than the 348, the 355 was an instant classic and sold over 9000 in six years. Saw debut of F1 paddleshift gearbox.
F355 Berlinetta: 3496cc V8, 375bhp, 183mph

F50
(1995-97)

Using plenty of F1 know-how in its construction and V12 engine tech, the F50 was even better to drive than the F40. With just 349 built, it's also a lot rarer.
F50: 4699cc V12, 520bhp, 202mph

550 Maranello // Barchetta Pininfarina **(1996-2002)**

Evoking the Daytona, Ferrari went front-engined for its brilliant new series-production flagship. Total built: 3083, plus 448 Barchettas with the useless soft top.
550 Maranello: 5474cc V12, 478bhp, 199mph

360 Modena // Spider
(1999-2005)

All-aluminium construction for the 355's successor. Most were specced with F1 paddleshift gearboxes – a sign of things to come. Biggest seller yet: 16,000-plus.
360 Modena: 3586cc V8, 395bhp, 180mph+

Enzo Ferrari
(2002-05)

As with the F50, Ferrari's new hypercar used F1 tech in its construction and drivetrain. Also saw first of the new 'F140' family of V12 engines. 400 built.
Enzo Ferrari: 5998cc V12, 660bhp, 217mph

575M Maranello
(2002-06)

Only minor styling tweaks compared with 550, but 575 did get more power, F1 gearbox option and adaptive suspension. Total built: 2056.
575M Maranello: 5748cc V12, 508bhp, 202mph

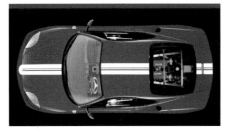

360 Challenge Stradale
(2003-04)

Inspired by the racers in the 360 Challenge series. Less weight than the standard 360, more power (by 20bhp) and tuned dynamics. Around 1200 were snapped up.
360 CS: 3586cc V8, 420bhp, 186mph

612 Scaglietti
(2004-2010)

Bigger than the 456M it replaced, which meant more room for rear passengers. No great looker, but surprisingly good to drive. Total built: 3025.
612 Scaglietti: 5748cc V12, 533bhp, 199mph

F430 // Spider
(2004-09)

Successor to 360 featured all-new 'F136' V8 and ramped up the tech even further, including E-diff electronically controlled rear diff (a road-car first).
F430: 4308cc V8, 483bhp, 196mph

599 GTB Fiorano
(2006-2012)

Replacing the 575M as Ferrari's series-production flagship, the 599 featured a version of the Enzo's V12 and more new tech, including F1-Trac traction control.
599 GTB: 5999cc V12, 611bhp, 205mph

430 Scuderia
(2007-2010)

Followed 360 Stradale formula of less weight, more power and racer attitude. As fast as an Enzo round Fiorano. Spider 16M version released in '08.
430 Scuderia: 4308cc V8, 503bhp, 198mph

California // California T
(2008-2017)

Front-mounted V8, 2+2 seating, folding hard-top. First generation had 483bhp; second-gen California T launched in 2014 used all-new twin-turbo V8.
California T: 3855cc tt V8, 553bhp, 196mph

458 Italia // Spider
(2009-2015)

Major reinvention of the mid-engined V8, with all-new structure, trick aero, seven-speed dual-clutch 'box and 4.5-litre version of F136 V8. A game-changer.
458 Italia: 4497cc V8, 562bhp, 202mph

599 GTO
(2010-12)

No racing link for this GTO, but the road version of the track-only 599XX was 100kg lighter than the GTB and faster than the Enzo at Fiorano. Only 599 built.
599 GTO: 5999cc V12, 661bhp, 208mph

FF
(2011-15)

Replacing 612 Scaglietti in the range, FF was first ever four-wheel-drive Ferrari. Room for four, a hatchback boot and 200mph-plus from huge F140-series V12.
FF: 6262cc V12, 651bhp, 208mph

F12 Berlinetta
(2013-17)

Replaced 599 GTB as mainstream flagship car. Laden with tech, including active aerodynamics and seven-speed dual-clutch transmission.
F12 Berlinetta: 6262cc V12, 730bhp, 211mph

458 Speciale // Speciale A
(2013-15)

A hardcore 458, with weight down and power up by 35bhp. Also a last hurrah for the naturally aspirated V8. Speciale A convertible launched in 2014 just as thrilling.
458 Speciale: 4497cc V8, 597bhp, 202mph+

LaFerrari // LaFerrari Aperta
(2013-18)

Dramatic range-topper, with up to 963bhp from its V12 and the KERS system. Just 500 built before production switched in 2016 to the open-top Aperta (210 built).
LaFerrari: 6262cc V12 + KERS, 963bhp, 217mph

488 GTB // Spider
(2015-19)

This entry in the long line of mid-engined V8s was set apart by its downsized twin-turbo engine, part of the F154 family, also found in the Lusso T.
488 GTB: 3902cc tt V8, 661bhp, 205mph

F12 TdF
(2016-17)

Track-focused version of F12 Berlinetta. Alarmingly fast, and slightly edgy on-limit handling added to the challenge. Production limited to 799.
F12 tdf: 6262cc V12, 769bhp, 211mph

GTC4 Lusso // Lusso T
(2016-2020)

FF refresh was so comprehensive that Ferrari renamed its 4WD four-seater the GTC4 Lusso. Twin-turbo V8 and rear-drive-only for the Lusso T, introduced in 2017.
GTC4 Lusso: 6282cc V12, 680bhp, 208mph

812 Superfast // GTS
(2017-)

Replaced F12 Berlinetta as Ferrari's production flagship, packing 789bhp. The Monza SP1 and SP2 speedsters share its mechanicals. Open-top GTS added in 2019.
812 Superfast: 6496cc V12, 789bhp, 211mph

Portofino // Portofino M
(2018-)

Replacement for the California T, with uprated version of the T's twin-turbo V8. Pokier Modificata (M) arrived in 2021 and shares engine tweaks with the Roma.
Portofino: 3855cc tt V8, 592bhp, 199mph

488 Pista // Spider
(2018-2020)

Road-racer boasting some remarkable chassis tech including the Ferrari Dynamic Enhancer that can make even a moderately able driver feel like a hero.
488 Pista: 3902cc tt V8, 710bhp, 211mph

F8 Tributo // Spider
(2019-)

The replacement for the 488 takes performance to another level, courtesy of the Pista's 710bhp twin-turbo engine and much of its trick aero, too.
F8 Tributo: 3902cc tt V8, 710bhp, 211mph

Roma
(2020-)

Sleek new GT based on the original Portofino but dramatically different in character, offering impressive dynamics as well as comfort and straight-line speed.
Roma: 3855cc tt V8, 611bhp, 199mph

SF90 Stradale // Spider
(2020-)

Hybrid hypercar is faster around Fiorano than LaFerrari – by a full second with the optional handing pack.
SF90 Stradale: 3990cc tt V8 + 3 electric motors, 986bhp, 211mph

812 Competizione // Aperta
(2021-)

A leaner, meaner, higher-revving version of the 812 Superfast, with an extra 30bhp. Open-top Aperta (599 units) will be scarcer than the hard-top (999 units).
812 Competizione: 6496cc V12, 819bhp, 211mph+

296 GTB
(2022-)

The first 'real' Ferrari with six cylinders will be rather more powerful than the little Dinos that preceded it.
296 GTB: 2992cc V6 + electric motor, 819bhp, 205mph+

FORZA ITALIA!

A multi-car track test at Anglesey Circuit brings out Ferrari's competitive streak

Words James Disdale

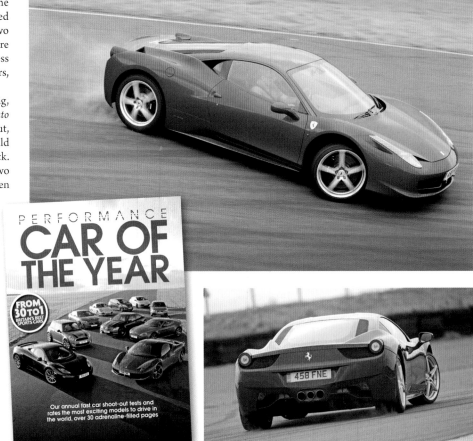

THE FERRARI engineer leaned into the cockpit of the 458 Italia and with a clenched fist beat the driver on the chest. 'De extra two tenths,' he said. 'They in 'ere.' Now the pressure was really on. Ferrari always means business when it comes to setting lap times in its cars, but today the stakes were higher than ever.

It was 2011 and we were at the rolling, corkscrewing Anglesey Circuit for the *Auto Express* Performance Car of the Year shoot-out, in which the ten best driver's machines would be pitted against one another and the clock. However, this year it was only really about two cars: the Ferrari 458 Italia and the McLaren 12C. Getting these two together had taken months of cajoling, but eventually both sides relented and so here we were, with the man in red psyching up our man at the wheel.

The moment was typical of the passion Ferrari demonstrated over the three days of the test. When I'd given the same chap a tour of the circuit, he'd turned to me and said: 'Eeet doesn't matter eef you crasha da car, justa make sure you go fastest.'

Ferrari's support effort reflected this attitude. McLaren's then-fledgling road car division wasn't the slick operation it is now, so the 12C was accompanied by a single technician with limited interest in the proceedings and a Tupperware lunchbox filled with cheese-and-pickle sandwiches. The men from Maranello came with engineers, enough tyres to keep the average Kwik Fit going for a month, and an Italian-registered 458 (the UK press car we'd used for photos wasn't to be used for lap timing) that was disgorged from an F1-spec transporter.

Senior road tester and former Formula Ford champ Owen Mildenhall was the man charged with setting the times. Ferrari first, and from the pit wall it sounded like Owen was on it, the V8 howling, Pirellis chirupping. After a handful of laps he set a best of 59.5sec around the National circuit. Next up, the 12C. It took precision and commitment to drag a quick

Above
The car that readers saw in photos wasn't the one that did the lap times at Anglesey; that car came from Italy especially for the track test, with a full support crew.

time out of this high-tech missile, but the result was an impressive 59.3sec. So it was victory to McLaren. The men from Maranello, however, were having none of it, and Owen was sent back out in the 458, returning with a 59.4 and a belief that this was the best he could do – which is where we began our story.

With the pep talk over and new tyres fitted, the Italia exited the pits one more time. You could see Owen's extra intent in the car's body language as it used every last inch of track. Five laps later he was back, having logged a 59.2. The Italians were elated, high-fiving and hugging. And McLaren? Their man shrugged and returned to his sandwiches. *End*

'It was victory to McLaren. The men from Maranello, however, were having none of it'